Beyond the Traps

A Journey to enlightened living

A wisdom book to shape your destiny

Mandakini Tomar

ISBN
Hardcase 979-8-89673-726-1
Paperback 979-8-89588-611-3

DEDICATION

I dedicate this book, first and foremost, to Lord Krishna. His teachings, guidance, and response to my prayers have been transformative, illuminating my path and turning my life toward purpose and fulfillment. Through His wisdom, I have found strength in challenges and clarity in uncertainty, allowing me to embrace my journey with renewed faith and resolve.

Through His divine wisdom, I found inspiration and clarity that propelled me to write, create, and help people through my words. Each step of my journey has been illuminated by His wisdom, urging me to convey the lessons I've learned. The Divine presence has guided my pen, turning my thoughts into words and empowering me to reach out to others. In every page, I seek to honor the blessings and fulfill the purpose that has been set for me.

The last few chapters are completely Devi Kripa, so I dedicate this book to the lotus feet of Goddess Triyambake, for her divine blessings and strength.

I dedicate this work to my grandfather, the late Shri Rajendra Singh Tomar, for his blessings.

Contents

Illumine your mind with life-changing questions.

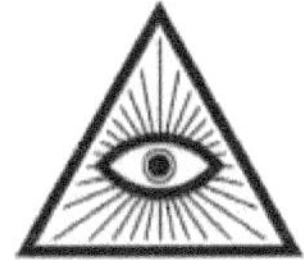

WHO

1. Who is a superior person?

2. Who is a happy person?

3. Who should we associate with?

4. Who is an awake person?

5. Who is a prudent person?

6. Who is a strong-minded person?

7. Who is free from pain?

HOW

1. How to judge the character of a person?

2. How to discover your true self?

3. How to be hopeful in stressful times?

4. How to keep moving and growing?

5. How to deal with disappointment or hopelessness?

6. How to deal with people who don't value you?

7. How can I align my actions with my spiritual values?

Preface

Sometimes we fall into the trap of doing something, thinking, or behaving in a way that is not wise or sensible. Our mind is wandering and looking for answers about life and ways of living life that can illuminate our mind. The questions that we ask are simple, but the answers are not so simple.

TRAP:

- **T**ransform Failures
- **R**ecognize Traps
- **A**chieve Awareness
- **P**rove Resilience

1. **Identifying Life's Traps**: The book begins by identifying common traps that people fall into, such as self-doubt, fear of failure, and resistance to change. Through vivid storytelling and real-life examples, Mandakini Tomar illustrates how these traps can hinder personal growth and fulfillment.

2. **Navigating Challenges**: Each chapter focuses on a specific trap and provides practical strategies for overcoming it. Readers are guided through a step-by-step process that includes recognizing the trap, understanding its impact, and employing effective methods to transcend it. This section emphasizes resilience, adaptability, and self-discovery.

3. **Embracing Transformation**: Once readers have navigated these challenges, the book explores the transformative effects of overcoming them. It delves into how facing and surpassing significant obstacles can lead to greater self-awareness, emotional intelligence, and spiritual growth.

4. **Living with Enlightenment**: The final section of the book focuses on pertinent questions related to life and mistakes in the sections of 'Who' and 'How' that spark reflection and illuminate you with wisdom. It offers guidance on how to maintain newfound perspectives and continue personal growth. The author provides practices for sustaining enlightenment, including mindfulness, reflection, and purpose-driven living.

This book empowers readers to embrace their mistakes and failures, understand their life traps, and transform their experiences into powerful lessons. The book provides a hopeful and proactive approach to overcoming obstacles, encouraging readers to turn their missteps into opportunities for profound personal growth and lasting change.

It is more than just a guide to navigating errors and avoiding pitfalls; it is a transformative journey toward a more fruitful and enlightened life. The author combines practical wisdom with spiritual insights to offer a comprehensive approach to personal and professional growth.

It helps readers navigate the complexities of life's mistakes and traps, steering them toward a more fruitful and divinely inspired existence.

The book begins by illuminating common traps that many people fall into, such as the trap of not giving any priority to yourself, the trap of overworking and ignoring health & other crucial aspects, the trap of not understanding the amazing power of the human mind and thoughts, the trap of not taking charge of your feelings or emotions after going through a bad experience or sadness, etc. All these traps hold you back in life, impacting both personal and professional growth. Recognizing these traps is crucial, as awareness is the first step toward overcoming them. Ultimately, the practice of awareness transforms how individuals engage with their lives, leading to more thoughtful decisions and a greater sense of agency in shaping their own destiny. Through vivid storytelling and real-life examples, I have illustrated how these traps hinder fulfillment and personal development. Combining practical wisdom with spiritual insights, this book will provide a hopeful and proactive approach to overcoming obstacles, encouraging readers to turn their traps into opportunities for profound personal growth and lasting change.

The book serves as a beacon for those seeking to transform their experiences into lasting wisdom and achieve a higher level of personal fulfillment. It is also for proactive people who want to avoid falling into these traps by being aware of them.

Each chapter focuses on a specific trap, providing practical strategies for overcoming these challenges. You will be guided through a step-by-step process that includes recognizing the trap, understanding its impact, and employing effective methods to transcend it.

Once readers have confronted these obstacles, the book delves into the transformative effects of overcoming them. It highlights how facing significant challenges can lead to greater self-awareness, emotional intelligence, and spiritual growth. The final chapter of the book provides profound answers to essential life questions about purpose, mistakes, and happiness, drawing on the wisdom of enlightened masters and sacred scriptures. It helps readers internalize these insights, encouraging reflection, mindfulness, and purpose-driven living as tools for personal growth and lasting fulfillment.

By addressing issues, you learn to actively work to transform your mindset, life, and behavior. This proactive approach allows you to break free from limiting patterns, embrace new experiences, and develop resilience to meet your destiny. What is Destiny?

Destiny can be understood as the culmination of your true self meeting your fullest potential. It represents the unique path you are meant to follow, shaped by your experiences, choices, and innate qualities. When you align your actions and values with your authentic self, you create a harmonious journey that leads to personal fulfillment and growth. Destiny isn't just about predetermined outcomes; it's about actively engaging with your passions and strengths, overcoming traps or obstacles, and embracing opportunities for transformation. In this sense, your destiny becomes a reflection of who you truly are and the heights you can reach when you fully embrace your potential. *It is a dynamic interplay between self-discovery, purpose, and the courage to pursue your dreams.* This book will guide you toward your real destiny and it's never too late to find it.

"You are never too old to set another goal or to dream a new dream."

C.S. Lewis

Trust me, it's never too late to take control of your destiny. People might judge based on their limited perspective, but only you know your true potential and what you're capable of achieving. With the right mindset and determination, you can always rewrite your story, no matter how challenging the past may seem. Start by identifying what holds you back. Start by identifying what traps you are entangled in, how to come out of them. Is it the fear of what others might think? Or perhaps a past failure that lingers in your mind? Acknowledge these feelings, but don't let them control you. Do not let others' opinions about you control you.

Now, envision the life you desire. Every small step you take is a victory, each decision a chance to reclaim your power. Embrace challenges as opportunities for growth, and remember that even the most successful people encountered life traps that threatened to hold them back. What distinguished them was their ability to recognize these traps and choose to rise above them. It's not about never falling; it's about rising each time you do.

In the Indian epic *Mahabharata*, Arjuna is initially paralyzed by doubt and moral confusion on the battlefield of Kurukshetra, torn between duty and personal feelings. This trap involves a struggle between conflicting duties, values, or emotions. In Arjuna's case, he is torn between his duty as a warrior (Kshatriya) to fight in the battle and his deep personal feelings of love and compassion for his family and friends on the opposing side. With guidance from Lord Krishna, he learns to overcome his inner conflicts and fears, embracing his destiny as a warrior. This illustrates the importance of seeking guidance and confronting one's fears to fulfill one's purpose. It teaches you that overcoming such life traps often requires introspection, clarity, and support.

"Beyond the Traps" is not just about overcoming challenges but about embracing the holistic transformation that follows to help you reach your highest good. It encourages readers to use their experiences to create a more fulfilling and enlightened life. **Seneca** said, "A good character, when established, is like a good rock. It does not easily get moved."

This speaks to the strength that comes from self-awareness and moral integrity. This book thus helps you in character building. "Character is destiny."

Heraclitus gave this piece of wisdom, suggesting that our inner awareness and choices shape the course of our lives and destiny.

Your dreams are waiting for you! Take that leap of faith today. Break free from the traps, embrace your journey, and pursue your destiny with courage and determination. The only thing stopping you is the belief that you can't. It's time to prove yourself wrong! You are capable, you are strong, and you are destined for greatness.

Go seize it!

Enjoy this journey where you are called by Divine Will to transform your mind to create clear, illumined thoughts, to lift the veils of illusion, and to release beliefs that do not serve you. Let your mind expand with this Will. Open to revelations, new awareness, perspectives, and insights. As you work with this will, Let your mind transform and become an illuminating light. Your thoughts become beautiful; you have higher, more loving, compassionate, focused, and clear thoughts. Your thoughts will carry you closer to enlightenment. Your mind will be a field of light for Divine Will to pour into. Your thoughts will be your soul's guidance, loving thoughts about you, other people, and the situations in your life.

Let your higher thoughts become more visible, thoughts that have come from the highest planes of light, enlightened thoughts that carry the energy of Divine Will. Let these new thoughts be like seeds that are beginning to sprout everywhere.

Enjoy your Illumined mind and the new vision!

"Your destiny is not a matter of chance; it is a matter of choice."

Don't Fall into the Traps

In the shadows where doubts may creep,

Life's traps lie waiting, silent and deep.

They whisper of fears that cloud your bright mind,

Distracting your journey with tempting smiles.

Don't fall into traps of self-doubt and dread,

Where dreams go to wither, and hopes are misled.

Recognize the fears that cloud your clear view,

For the path to your destiny starts right with you.

The trap of perfection, so shiny and bright,

Can keep you from moving, from taking your flight.

Embrace your mistakes; let them teach you and grow,

For in every misstep, there's wisdom to sow.

Beware the allure of chasing the wrong,

For fleeting distractions can lead you astray.

Stay true to your purpose; let passion be your guide.

In the journey of life, let authenticity reside.

The trap of comparison can dim your own spark,

Remember, your journey is uniquely your mark.

Celebrate your progress, no matter how small,

For each step is a victory, and you're destined to stand tall.

So rise above traps; let your spirit be free,

With courage and clarity, choose who you will be.

For life's greatest treasures await within your reach,

And the path to your destiny is yours to enrich.

Wisdom Behind the Sign

The sign for wisdom is the eye. It represents insight, knowledge, and understanding. "Coming out of traps" often means escaping difficult situations or overcoming obstacles. It signifies resilience and the ability to find freedom or clarity after being stuck. This journey can lead to newfound strength and understanding, allowing for personal growth and transformation. It can take us to a place of higher consciousness and enlightenment.

The crescent moon is often associated with wisdom and intuition. In the context of overcoming traps, it symbolizes the ability to see beyond the surface, to understand underlying patterns and motivations, and to navigate situations with foresight and discernment. The crescent moon represents the growing light of understanding that guides us through potentially dangerous or misleading paths. It signifies the ability to see beyond the immediate, to recognize subtle signs and warnings, and to ultimately escape the traps that others might fall into.

The dot below the crescent moon is a visual representation of creation. In Sufism, the dot represents the starting point of everything. It stands for completeness and perfection, symbolizing the first act of creation by the Divine. From this single dot, all directions and dimensions come into being. It shows that every creation begins with this important mark made by the Divine Pen.

If you want to reach out to me, connect with me on-

Instagram - mandakinitomar_

Website - *www.mandakinitomar.com*

Email - *mandakini.author@gmail.com*

I would love to connect with my lovely readers.

Post pictures and tag!

Acknowledgment

I would like to express my heartfelt gratitude to those who have supported me throughout this journey.

First and foremost, I thank my mother, Aradhana, and my father, Pradeep Singh Tomar, for their unwavering love and encouragement. Your belief in me has been my greatest motivation.

To my brother, Apoorv, thank you for your constant support and for always being there to uplift me.

I extend my sincere appreciation to the team at Notion Press Publishing, yet again, after my first book, for their professionalism and guidance in bringing this book to life.

I am deeply grateful to all my Gurus (especially Neem Karoli Baba whose Divine presence and guidance motivates me), teachers and elders for their invaluable blessings and wisdom. Your influence has shaped me in ways I cannot fully express.

Thank you all for being an integral part of this journey.

May we all continue to add miles to our journeys and live happy lives.

Embark on This Journey

Introduction: The Journey Through Life's Traps

Life is an intricate journey, full of twists and turns, highs and lows, and moments that test our resolve. Each step we take can bring us closer to our goals or lead us into traps that seem to impede our progress. These traps—whether they are self-neglect trap, trap of being too helpful, trap of trusting people easily etc.—are not merely obstacles; they are profound opportunities for growth and transformation.

The Nature of Life's Traps

Life's traps are often subtle and insidious, disguising themselves as comfort zones or temporary setbacks. They ensnare us with promises of safety or ease, only to leave us feeling stagnant and unfulfilled. For instance, self-doubt may whisper that we are not capable or worthy, causing us to hesitate or retreat from opportunities. Fear of failure can paralyze us, preventing us from taking risks that are essential for growth. Resistance to change keeps us anchored in familiar but limiting patterns, while procrastination steals our time and energy, delaying our dreams. Overconfidence, on the other hand, can lead to complacency, where we stop striving and settle for mediocrity.

The Purpose of Overcoming Challenges

Understanding and overcoming these traps is not about eliminating obstacles entirely; it's about transforming our relationship with them. Each trap offers a lesson, a chance to reflect on our behavior, beliefs, and patterns. When approached with awareness and intention, these challenges become powerful teachers. They reveal areas where we need to grow, adapt, and evolve.

Overcoming life's traps can lead to profound personal transformation. It's through the struggle and eventual triumph over these obstacles that we discover our true strength, resilience, and capacity for change. The process of confronting and transcending these traps often leads to greater self-awareness, emotional intelligence, and a deeper understanding of our purpose in life.

How Facing Obstacles Leads to Enlightenment

Enlightenment in this context refers to a state of clarity and insight that emerges from navigating life's traps. It's about gaining a higher perspective on our experiences and recognizing the interconnectedness of our actions, beliefs, and outcomes. When we overcome a trap, we often find ourselves transformed, not just in our approach to similar challenges in the future, but in our overall outlook on life.

This book, *Beyond the Traps: A journey to enlightened living*, is designed to guide you through this transformative journey and bring you closer to your destiny. It offers practical strategies for recognizing and addressing common traps, as well as profound insights into how these challenges can lead to a more enlightened and fulfilled life. Through a blend of personal stories, expert advice, and actionable techniques, you will learn how to navigate your obstacles, embrace your growth, and live a life aligned with your deepest values and aspirations.

As you embark on this journey, remember that overcoming life's traps is not a destination but a continuous process. It's about developing the resilience to face new challenges, the wisdom to learn from your experiences, and the courage to transform your life in meaningful ways. By the end of this book, you will have embarked on a transformative journey that equips you with the tools to recognize and navigate the emotional and psychological traps that have hindered your growth. Each chapter will guide you through self-reflection, helping you identify limiting beliefs and patterns that have kept you in a cycle of dissatisfaction. As you confront these obstacles, you will also discover actionable strategies and insights that illuminate a path toward a more enlightened and purposeful existence. By integrating these lessons into your daily life, you will cultivate resilience, deepen your understanding of yourself, and ultimately embrace a more fulfilling way of being, characterized by clarity, intention, strong character, and an unwavering sense of purpose.

"Every obstacle is a doorway to growth; step through with courage, and you will find your true self waiting on the other side."

The Trap of Not Learning from Mistakes: Repeating Patterns

The Repeat Offender Trap

"The true measure of wisdom is not in avoiding mistakes, but in how we respond to them and choose not to repeat them."

There are so many times that you say to yourself, "Oh, I will never do this again. I will never fall into this trap of repeating my patterns of behavior which are harmful for me or which go against me," only to find yourself committing the same mistake again. This time I am not going to waste time as it cost me a lot in the past. This time I am not going to listen to what other people say about my life choices and continue doing what my heart tells me to. This time I am not going to fall into a superficial relationship. This time I am not going to repeat the mistake of trusting people too easily. These are some common mistakes that we make as humans. As humans, you tend to err. Committing mistakes is alright since they teach you what not to be, how not to behave, or what generally goes against you. If you are aware and observant enough about your patterns, you will be aware of the lesson hidden behind the mistakes. Repeated mistakes often stem from a mix of unresolved internal issues, habitual behaviors, lack of self-awareness, ineffective learning, external pressures, and emotional responses.

Mistakes are a part of the learning process. Yet, if you choose to live in a deep slumber, not observant enough of your actions, it can really cost you in more ways than one. *Smart is the one who makes a mistake, learns from it, and never makes that same mistake again.* You can live your life beautifully if you choose to reflect upon the learning from the mistakes you committed in the past and decide to cultivate wisdom to not repeat them again and again. For this, you need to identify –

- Why do you keep going the same route again and again?

- What are your triggers?

- What kind of people do you need to avoid?

- Are there any distractions in your life that are costing you a lot?

- Are you aware of your natural instincts?

- Do you often overlook or dismiss warning signs?

- Do you rely on impulse or emotions rather than logical reasoning and thorough analysis?

Reflect on these questions.

Life doesn't spare anyone and gives hard knocks to everyone, the most noble and the most courageous, the saintliest none is spared. *The Universe is testing you at each stage. Sometimes you pass the test, but sometimes you make mistakes by falling into the trap of your triggers.* The truth remains that the faster you learn from your mistakes, the faster you learn to climb the ladder of happiness.

Suppose Arun is an individual who enjoys gambling. Despite experiencing repeated losses and financial strain from his gambling habits, he continues to gamble regularly. Each time he loses, he promises himself that he will stop or change his strategy. However, his excitement and desire to win back his losses lead him to repeat the same behavior over and over. Arun fails to engage in genuine self-reflection about why his gambling strategy is failing. Peer pressure or a desire to fit in with friends who gamble might contribute to his continued behavior, making it harder for him to break free from his cycle of mistakes. He might focus on the belief that "just one more try" will turn things around, rather than examining the fundamental flaws in his approach.

His behavior is foolish because he is trapped in a cycle of repeating the same mistake without learning from it. His failure to adapt, reflect, or take meaningful action to change his behavior highlights a lack of wisdom and awareness. This persistent error not only continues to lead to negative outcomes but also demonstrates a fundamental misunderstanding of how to address and correct one's mistakes.

In life, if you learn too late, then it is only going to fill your soul with remorse that you just missed climbing the ladder of happiness. Realizing you've made mistakes and not learned from them earlier can bring feelings of regret and guilt. This can weigh heavily on your conscience and impact your self-esteem, leading to a sense of loss or missed opportunities.

So, stop, take a step back, and take a look whether you are a slow learner or a fast learner. Start by taking a firm resolve to not repeat your mistakes. *Mistakes can lead to situations where you can apply your newfound wisdom, helping you to evolve and better understand yourself. But do not make the same mistake again and again.*

For example, if you touch a hot plate even after repeated warnings and burn yourself, then your lesson is to follow the warnings and be more cautious and not negligent. You learn to obey directions. Only lamenting over your mistakes won't suffice; you should think and reflect on what the Universe is trying to teach you. Where are you going wrong? Why are you falling into the same loop of mistakes again and again?

What is it that needs to be corrected: a behavior pattern, your way of thinking, your decision-making styles (emotional, impulsive, or rational), lack of boundaries in your life, too much empathy, being too nice, lack of confidence, people-pleasing behavior, not taking a stand for yourself, etc. You should extract lessons from each mistake. Consider what went wrong, what you could have done differently, and how to apply this insight in future situations.

Many of our behaviors are driven by unconscious beliefs formed in early childhood or even past experiences. These beliefs can create mental scripts that dictate how you perceive yourself and the world, leading you to repeat similar mistakes.

In spiritual traditions like Hinduism, Buddhism, and certain New Age beliefs, Karma is seen as the universal law of cause and effect. *When you fail to learn from your mistakes, you will find yourself stuck in karmic loops, repeating the same situations or encountering similar challenges until you decide to break free by understanding and addressing the root cause.*

When you don't learn from them, the same situations tend to arise in life repeatedly. These could manifest as recurring relationship issues, financial struggles, health problems, or career setbacks. Each repetition is an opportunity to recognize the pattern and understand the deeper lesson hidden within it. I remember my mother telling me, *"Before anything major happens, the Universe always gives us signs."* These signs, often referred to as "synchronicities," "omens," or "intuitive nudges," are believed to be messages from a higher power, the Universe, or our higher selves.

So, you must understand that certain people or situations might trigger strong emotional reactions in you that lead to repeating mistakes, like anger, fear, jealousy, or attachment. These triggers can be karmic tests, probably encouraging you to learn to respond with awareness and balance rather than react impulsively. *In archery, if you rush to release the arrow without proper aim and preparation, it will miss the target.* Similarly, in life, actions taken hastily without careful thought and focus are more likely to miss the intended goal.

Sometimes, the Universe signals an upcoming change through shifts in our personal relationships, jobs, or other circumstances. For instance, unexpected conflicts, endings, or new connections can be indications that a significant transformation is on the horizon. Relationships, whether familial, romantic, or social, are often a significant area where karmic patterns will play out. Repeating similar dynamics with different people (e.g., constantly attracting controlling partners or manipulative friends) suggests a karmic lesson that needs to be learned, such as **self-love**, **setting boundaries**, or **learning empathy**.

Every mistake is an opportunity to develop virtues such as patience, humility, empathy and resilience. By understanding the root causes of mistakes and actively working to transform them, individuals can break free from karmic cycles and move toward higher states of consciousness.

How to Come Out of the Trap

"Growth begins where repetition ends; embrace the lessons of your past to forge a wiser future."

Breaking Free from Karmic Patterns: The cyclic nature of life, the spiral, always brings you the opportunity for a new re-signification (giving a new meaning or purpose). The question is, are you willing to take a quantum leap, or are you repeating the same cycle?

To break free from karmic patterns, one must:

Cultivate Awareness: Recognize recurring patterns in your life where you find yourself stuck in similar situations and reflect on the underlying lessons they are trying to present. The first step in breaking free from any repetitive pattern is awareness. Without recognizing that a pattern exists, it is impossible to change it. You should start by reflecting on areas of your life where you notice recurring themes or problems. Journaling, meditation, or talking with a trusted friend can help you identify these patterns.

Questions to consider include:

- What situations or types of people do I find myself repeatedly encountering?
- Are there specific emotions or reactions that frequently surface in my life?
- What beliefs or thoughts do I hold that might be contributing to these patterns?

Developing self-awareness requires honesty and openness to facing potentially uncomfortable truths. Don't hide from yourself; embrace the clarity that comes with seeing things as they truly are. It is essential to approach this process with compassion and a non-judgmental attitude.

- **Start** Regular meditation, journaling, or introspection that can help you uncover subconscious beliefs and behaviors. You can **Seek Guidance** from spiritual teachers, therapists, your confidant, or guides who can provide insights into the karmic lessons you need to learn.

- **Forgive and Release**: Letting go of past hurts and forgiving oneself and others is crucial to breaking free from karmic cycles. Forgiving others, and even oneself, allows for the release of emotional blockages that can hinder spiritual progress and well-being. You have a chance to free yourself from the emotional and mental turmoil that comes with holding onto grudges. This peace creates positive karma, reflected in a more harmonious and balanced life.

- **Create New Positive Patterns**: Make conscious efforts to create new, positive habits, responses, and behaviors to replace old patterns. *Creating new patterns for good karma is about cultivating a lifestyle that is rooted in kindness, integrity, and conscious living.* Each positive action, no matter how small, contributes to a ripple effect that not only improves our own lives but also positively impacts the world around us. By consistently practicing these principles, we can build a reservoir of good karma that supports spiritual growth, happiness, and fulfillment.

- Mantra – Change habits, seek advice, or set up safeguards.

The Light of Wisdom

If you want to know how to best deal with mistakes, then you should turn to God. God speaks through scriptures. The only sure-fire way is to turn to God. Acknowledge your mistake and ask Him to help you by being your guiding hand. Ultimately, forgiveness is about letting go and surrendering to a higher power, trusting that everything happens for a reason and that every experience—pleasant or painful—is an opportunity for growth. This surrender creates an openness to receive positive karma and blessings in abundance.

Remember when you surrender, He will make good out of your unintentional mistakes or mistakes committed due to unawareness. He will use those mistakes to catalyze your growth. He is the one who can make beauty from the ashes. He will turn out things magically and make you grasp the wisdom and truth. He will intervene and correct you at the right moment just when you are about to repeat the same mistakes which affect your soul and life. **"No temptation has overtaken you except what is common to mankind. And God is faithful; he will not let you be tempted beyond what**

you can bear. But when you are tempted, he will also provide a way out so that you can endure it" (1 Corinthians 10:13)

He will make your heart filled with self-love, forgiveness, compassion, and in complete awe of his direction. Like a shepherd, he will guide you to come out of this trap. *You will learn to work on yourself, you will know yourself better, and you will become aware of the impact of your actions.* All this wisdom is nothing but his guidance to lead you onto the right path into your future as a wiser and humbled person. So, bow down before Him. He will redeem you and help you not fall into the pitfalls to make wise decisions.

The LORD upholds all who are falling and raises up all who are bowed down.
- Psalm 145:14

Mindful Wisdom of the Buddha

Buddhism emphasizes **mindfulness** and **awareness** as crucial tools to break free from the cycle of **samsara**: the endless cycle of birth, death, and rebirth influenced by karma. Repeating mistakes is seen as a result of ignorance (**avidya**) and attachment (**tanha**). The **Dhammapada**, one of the most widely read and studied Buddhist scriptures, states:

> **"An ignorant man is a fool. A wise man is never a fool, for he is always alert to avoid repetition of past mistakes."** (Dhammapada 63).

This verse underscores the significance of wisdom and mindfulness in avoiding the recurrence of mistakes. Being "ever alert" is akin to being fully present and aware in each moment. To be "ever alert" is to cultivate awareness in every moment, staying mindful and conscious of your choices. This kind of presence not only helps you grow but also prevents you from falling into the traps of ignorance and repetition.

The Jewish practice of **Yom Kippur**, the Day of Atonement, is dedicated to reflection, repentance, and forgiveness. It is a time to reflect on the past year, recognize mistakes, and commit to change. Yom Kippur is a day filled with deep spiritual meaning and symbolism. Its core themes include:

- **Repentance (Teshuva)**: Yom Kippur encourages sincere self-reflection and taking responsibility for one's actions. Teshuva is a process of turning inward, acknowledging mistakes, and committing to positive change. This process of introspection and renewal offers an opportunity to realign ourselves with our values and purpose, fostering both personal growth and spiritual healing. It's a powerful reminder that the path to growth is through honesty and accountability.

- **Forgiveness (Selichot)**: Seeking and granting forgiveness is a key component of Yom Kippur. It is a time to forgive others and ask for forgiveness from those we may have hurt or wronged, as well as seeking divine forgiveness.

- **Renewal and Rebirth**: Yom Kippur offers a spiritual "clean slate." By engaging in sincere repentance and self-examination, individuals have the opportunity to start anew with a fresh outlook and commitment to living ethically. It's a powerful opportunity to re-align with your values, rebuild broken connections, and strive for a more compassionate, purposeful existence in the year ahead.

"To escape the trap of repeating mistakes, we must first commit to understanding them and choosing a different path."

The Trap of Not Giving Any Priority to Yourself: Sacrificing Your Own Happiness

The Self-Neglect Trap

To create a balanced life and a content life, which we all strive for, you have to avoid falling into the trap of not making yourself a priority. Often in life, you are so engrossed in your relationships, work, and outward world that you forget to

1. Love yourself a little.

2. Focus on yourself.

3. Live for yourself or

4. Live by being true to your deepest desires.

5. Take rest to contemplate and for the renewal of the mind, time and again.

The concept of prioritizing oneself can be deeply intertwined with understanding one's true self, purpose, and connection to a higher reality or the divine. When you forget to connect with yourself, when you miss out on doing things that you feel in your heart to be right, you fail to give priority to yourself. *Prolonged disconnection from your true self will result in emotional strain, such as anxiety, frustration, or sadness.* This emotional stress arises from the gap between your true self and the persona you present to the world. This disconnect often manifests as a sense of unease, dissatisfaction, or confusion. How can you expect to connect with the Divine when you are uneasy, dissatisfied, or confused? How can you expect to connect with the higher power or your higher self when you are living inauthentically? I have seen a lot of people who struggle with presenting different personalities or personas depending on their environment and audience. They wear masks to fit in with various social or professional contexts. For example, they may act one way at work, another way with friends, and yet another way in family settings. *Living inauthentically, or not true to your values, can diminish your overall sense of fulfillment and joy.* Only by aligning with your true self can you build deeper connections, enhance personal fulfillment, and achieve a more cohesive and authentic life. All this requires effort. Effort of giving time to yourself and nurturing your true self.

There is too much noise in the outward world. Everyone has to say something or the other. People have their judgments. You will be pulled out in all directions if you keep trying to listen to everyone else. Either you will be busy judging someone else or afraid to be judged by people. In the entire process of listening to everyone around you… what you forget is that it is necessary to listen to your heart too. You don't prioritize your truest desires…the deep desires of your heart. I ask you, why aren't you your priority? Don't you owe yourself that much love and kindness? Don't you love yourself? Are you not important? **Just as a garden in a busy city serves as a peaceful retreat from the hustle and bustle, creating a personal space or routine dedicated to self-care helps you escape the noise and focus on your well-being.** So, create that space where you prioritize yourself sans outside noise.

"Discover who you are, embrace who you are, cherish who you are, and the right friendships and love will naturally follow." If you keep on putting others first and sacrificing your own happiness, you will be left with nothing but guilt or remorse. If you keep looking for validation from others, then you will be in for a long haul. If you keep wasting your energy to please everyone, then you will be disappointed. *No matter what you do, someone will feel disgruntled by the actions you take, choices you make.* All you would be left with is guilt of not answering your soul calling and life just slipped away.

You will feel as if you missed out on something, giving you a sense of void. You will realize that nurturing your soul, taking care of yourself, listening to your heart, and fulfilling your desires was not selfish but necessary. It was necessary so that you could give your best to the world out there. I am sure you don't want to go on that guilt trip. If not, then come out of this trap right now. Right now is all you have. If you want to live life the right way, do the right things, do things you are passionate about, follow your interests, follow your heart and soul, prioritize your desires too. You should break free from the trap of neglecting yourself by prioritizing your own needs and dreams with the same urgency you offer to others; only then will you truly live the life your soul is calling for.

Do not ever sacrifice who you are deep down inside. "In the face of external pressures, never sacrifice your inner essence; preserving who you are inside is the path to living a life of integrity and passion." **I urge you to guard your inner essence with unwavering resolve; it is the heart of your identity and the source of your true power. Never sacrifice your inner essence; preserving who you are inside is the path to living a life of integrity and passion.** It is a statement with a lot of depth. So, please honor yourself enough to be bold enough to stay authentic on your path of life.

Learn to Balance Action with Contemplation

This balance is essential for maintaining inner harmony and effectiveness in one's duties. There is no use in living a life of conformity; go beyond it and put yourself first because if you won't, then no one else will. It is not a selfish desire but rather a desire to give back to others from a place of abundance whereby you are radiating and beaming with love, happiness, and good intentions. Nurturing yourself by prioritizing yourself is not selfish but rather necessary for personal development and resilience. Even scriptures guide us to guard our hearts, renew our minds, and take care of our bodies. The body and mind are like a sacred temple. Just as plants need water to flourish, your well-being requires care and nurturing. Neglect them, and they will wither; nourish them, and they will thrive.

THE SAP AND THE ROOT

Being is the basis of all living, just as without the sap and root, there would be no tree. If we can take care of the sap, the whole tree will be taken care of. Similarly, if we can take care of **Being**, the whole field of thinking and doing will be taken care of.

(Maharishi Mahesh)

By caring for your essence—your Being—your thoughts and actions will naturally fall into harmony. In life, you need to cultivate the habit of giving yourself the most precious gift, and what is that gift?

It is time. *Time is the most precious gift.* Time is a finite resource, and how we choose to spend it can deeply influence our happiness, growth, and well-being. Ensure that you allocate time for work, leisure, and rest. You need a few moments to keep yourself centered. Krishna's teachings include the concept of detachment (vairagya) from material desires and outcomes. Giving time to yourself involves finding balance and focusing on your inner state rather than external achievements or possessions. Lord Krishna advises Arjuna to engage in disciplined practice (sadhana) and meditation to attain self-realization. Regular time spent in meditation is seen as essential for calming the mind and aligning with one's higher self.

Even Jesus Christ spent time alone in prayer. Jesus used his time alone to reflect on his mission and purpose. In the wilderness, before starting his public ministry, he fasted and prayed for forty days (Matthew 4:1-11). This period of solitude was essential for understanding his calling and preparing for the challenges ahead.

- **Gaining Perspective**: Solitude allows for deep reflection and gaining clarity on one's goals and direction. It provides space to assess one's path, make thoughtful decisions, and seek deeper understanding.

- **Avoiding Crowds**: Jesus sometimes withdrew from the crowds to avoid distraction and maintain focus on his mission. For example, in Mark 6:31, Jesus tells his disciples, **"Come with me by yourselves to a quiet place and get some rest."** This retreat was necessary to escape the constant demands and noise of public life.

- **Reducing Overwhelm**: Time alone helps reduce the noise and distractions of everyday life, allowing you to focus on what truly matters and manage stress effectively.

By retreating from the demands of daily life, Jesus was able to reconnect with God, prepare for his mission and find strength.

Divine Wisdom

As per scriptures, God's spirit dwells in you, and it is your duty to take care of it. In Hindu scriptures, the concept that the divine spirit dwells within every individual is a profound and central teaching. This idea underscores the belief in the divine presence within all living beings and highlights the potential for spiritual realization and enlightenment.

- **Divine Presence**: In the Bhagavad Gita, Lord Krishna reveals that He resides within the hearts of all beings. In Chapter 10, Verse 20, Krishna states, "I am the Self, O Gudakesha, seated in the hearts of all creatures. I am the beginning, the middle, and the end of all beings."

- **Chandogya Upanishad**: This text contains teachings that emphasize the presence of the divine within the self, stating that the essence of the divine is present in the innermost part of every being.

All this wisdom points toward self-awareness, introspection, and spiritual practices aimed at recognizing and connecting with the divine presence within oneself. Once you connect, you have to take care of it just like how you take care of a precious thing. You can only take care of it when you focus on yourself and are aware enough. The awareness gone, it slips. Hinduism guides you to strive for self-transformation since as human beings you are subject to the modifications of nature. Since you are a manifestation of the Universe, it is also your duty to focus on and nourish yourself both physically and mentally to make progress in life.

The Bible teaches you - Do not conform to the pattern of this world, but be transformed by the renewing of your mind. Then you will be able to test and approve what God's will is, His good, pleasing, and perfect will.

How do you renew your mind? The answer by dedicating time to yourself and cultivating habits that promote mental clarity, emotional balance, and spiritual growth.

Renewing your mind by giving time to yourself is key to emerging from the trap of neglecting yourself amidst chaos. It involves taking intentional steps to reclaim your time and prioritize your well-being. Here's how you can break free from this cycle and begin giving yourself the attention and care you deserve:

1. **Recognize the Importance of Self-Care**

   - **Acknowledge the Need**: Understand that self-care is not a luxury but a necessity. Recognizing that neglecting yourself impacts your overall health and effectiveness is the first step toward change.

   - **Shift Your Mindset**: Reframe self-care as an essential part of your productivity and well-being, rather than something to be done only when time allows.

2. **Set Boundaries**

   - **Define Limits**: Establish clear boundaries between work and personal time. Create designated times for relaxation and self-care that you stick to, even amidst a busy schedule.

   - **Communicate Boundaries**: Let others know your limits respectfully, so they understand and support your need for personal time.

3. **Prioritize and Plan**

   - **Create a Schedule**: Plan your day or week to include dedicated time for self-care. Use a planner or digital calendar to block out time for activities that nurture your well-being.

   - **Prioritize Tasks**: Focus on what truly matters and let go of less important tasks. Use prioritization techniques like the Eisenhower Matrix to identify and address your most critical responsibilities.

4. **Practice Mindfulness and Presence**

   o **Mindfulness Techniques**: Engage in mindfulness practices to help you stay present and reduce stress. Techniques such as deep breathing, meditation, and body scans can help ground you in the moment.

   o **Stay Present**: Focus on one task at a time to avoid feeling overwhelmed. Being present can help you manage chaos more effectively and make time for yourself.

5. **Create Personal Time**

   o **Schedule Breaks**: Incorporate short breaks throughout your day to recharge. Even brief moments of rest can prevent burnout and improve your productivity.

   o **Designate "Me Time"**: Set aside specific times each week solely for activities that you enjoy and that rejuvenate you, such as reading, walking, or hobbies.

6. **Learn to Say No**

   o **Evaluate Requests**: Assess whether additional commitments align with your priorities and values. Politely decline tasks or invitations that would overextend you.

   o **Practice Assertiveness**: Communicate your limits clearly and assertively, without feeling guilty. It's okay to prioritize your own needs.

7. **Develop Healthy Routines**

   o **Daily Rituals**: Establish daily routines that include self-care activities, such as exercise, healthy eating, and adequate sleep. Consistent routines can help you maintain balance.

   o **Self-Care Rituals**: Incorporate small rituals that promote relaxation, such as a morning meditation, evening reflection, or a weekly pampering session.

8. **Seek Support**

   o **Talk to Others**: Share your struggles with friends, family, or a therapist. Talking about your challenges can provide relief and practical advice.

   o **Join Support Groups**: Engage with groups or communities that offer encouragement and share similar experiences. Support from others can help you feel less isolated.

9. **Reflect and Adjust**

   o **Regular Check-Ins**: Periodically reflect on your self-care practices and their effectiveness. Adjust your routines and strategies as needed to ensure they continue to meet your needs.

   o **Celebrate Progress**: Acknowledge and celebrate the positive changes you make. Recognizing your efforts reinforces the importance of taking time for yourself.

10. **Incorporate Relaxation Techniques**

   o **Stress Reduction**: Use relaxation techniques such as yoga, progressive muscle relaxation, or listening to calming music to manage stress and foster a sense of calm.

   o **Creative Outlets**: Engage in creative activities that help you unwind and express yourself, such as drawing, writing, or playing music.

11. **Reevaluate Your Priorities**

   o **Assess Your Goals**. Periodically reassess your personal and professional goals. Ensure that they align with your values and allow you to maintain a healthy balance.

   o **Adjust Expectations**: Be realistic about what you can achieve within a given timeframe. Adjust your expectations to avoid overcommitting and to protect your well-being.

By implementing these strategies, you can break free from the cycle of neglecting yourself and create a more balanced, fulfilling life. Prioritizing your own well-being amidst chaos will not only enhance your quality of life, but also improve your ability to handle challenges effectively.

Universe starts helping you - Interconnectedness of Self-awareness, Well-being, and Universal support

When you make a conscious effort to prioritize yourself and create a balanced, fulfilling life, the Universe responds in supportive and synchronistic ways. This concept, often rooted in spiritual and philosophical beliefs, suggests that aligning your actions with your true self can lead to positive outcomes and opportunities. *When you sail with a well-prepared ship and a clear course, the ocean responds by offering smoother sailing, favorable winds, and navigable waters.* Similarly, when you align with your true self and invest in your well-being, the Universe often provides supportive conditions, guidance, and opportunities that help you progress.

"When you honor your true self and invest in your well-being, the Universe aligns its rhythm with your own, guiding you toward abundance and purpose."

The Trap of Overworking and Ignoring Health & Other Crucial Aspects

The Burnout Trap

"Don't get so busy making a living that you forget to make a life."
Don't wear yourself out trying to get rich. Be wise enough to know when to quit.
Proverb 23:4 NLT

Balance in life is so important. A lot of people struggle to find balance in life. *Remember, you work to live and not live to work.* Time is limited, and your priorities are many. Sometimes you will focus on one area of life and forget others totally, thinking that it might give you satisfaction, only to realize later that you completely ignored or missed out on some crucial parts of your life. Still, people keep falling into this trap of working too hard and facing burnout time after time. Work should enable you to live well, not dominate your life. Just as an orchestra needs all its sections to perform at their best to create a beautiful symphony, a well-balanced life requires attention to all its components and not just work.

When you pay attention to all parts of your life and avoid overemphasizing one area, you create a more harmonious and fulfilling existence. Just as a well-conducted orchestra creates a beautiful and balanced symphony, a well-balanced life allows each aspect to contribute to a richer and more satisfying experience.

There is constant pressure to do well socially and economically, which leads one to fall into the trap of throwing themselves into work like crazy. There is no time to eat food properly or attend family functions, spend time with friends, a partner, or children. A lot of people burn themselves out by working too much. Of course, there is no substitute for success other than working. Being competitive and successful is much needed and called for. But what is not called for is that you ignore other big commitments like health, whether physical or mental, and relationships.

Sometimes people work too much to avoid something personal, to fill an emotional gap or fill a vacuum. Work becomes a distraction from dealing with personal issues or emotions. Keeping busy can prevent someone from confronting problems or feelings they'd rather avoid. They are just too controlling and fearful to even let go of work for a few days. A fear of losing opportunity and losing control over business persists. *Sometimes it is better to be a little easy going for your own betterment. Sometimes, a lighter touch is just what's needed.* Work can definitely be a great way to stay engaged and productive, but it's also important to let yourself relax and enjoy life. Balancing work with downtime, hobbies, and time with loved ones can help keep things in perspective and make everything more enjoyable.

Rumi, a famous Sufi poet, said, "Let the beauty we love be what we do" (Rumi). This reflects the idea that our work should be aligned with our inner values and not overwhelm other aspects of life. *True balance comes from understanding and aligning with the natural flow of life, rather than pushing oneself to extremes.*

In his work "Nicomachean Ethics," Aristotle argued that while wealth is necessary for a good life, it is not sufficient for happiness. He believed that true fulfillment comes from living a life of virtue and developing meaningful relationships. For Aristotle, happiness (eudaimonia) is achieved through living in accordance with virtue and reason, rather than through the pursuit of material wealth. *Money can open doors to many opportunities and comforts, but it can't replace the intangible things that really enrich our lives, like meaningful relationships, love, and time.* These are often what give life its depth and joy. Cultivating strong connections with people, finding love, and making the most of our time with those we care about can bring a sense of fulfillment and happiness that money alone can't provide. How do you find balance between pursuing financial goals and nurturing these other important aspects of life?

Enjoy the process of working rather than making it a burdensome process for your body and soul. **You have to remind yourself that earning money is a part of life, not your entire life.** Money surely can buy you all the luxuries and is necessary to give you comforts, but money can't buy you time. *If you don't have time to enjoy those comforts or use that money efficiently to pursue your other goals, what is the use?* There has to be a fine balance in life.

You need time to use that money to travel, to experience different cuisines, feel the sunny weather, enjoy a walk by the beach, or spend time with your children explaining to them the beauty of life. When you are in your 20s or mid-30s, it is going to be easier for you to focus more on work because other commitments are not huge and liabilities aren't as significant. A too materialistic approach, as called in scriptures 'Maya', is going to make you delusional because you are in a mode of passion and ignorance. *But as you progress in life or get older, you should start focusing on other areas of life and prioritizing things.* There are higher goals in life too. Aristotle, one of the greatest Greek thinkers, said that all virtue in life is achieved by **"maintaining the golden mean"**. This means that, in order to find happiness, people should always strive for a balance between two extremes. In order to find happiness and live life contently, you should strive to find the Golden Mean. This is the key.

What is the Perfect Recipe for Suffering in Life?

If you observe carefully in life, you suffer whenever you do excess of something. You tend to lose balance and will keep on going in circles rather than going straight. *Without balance, you won't be able to soar high in life.* If you are excessively emotional, you will suffer and lose your center. That is why it is called being emotionally unbalanced. If you are excessively practical, you will suffer due to a lack of emotional connection. Both scenarios are harmful. Similarly, when it comes to work, if you go to extremes, you are bound to suffer. It will sap your energy and well-being. *Going to extremes in life means you are only going to go far away from your center.* You will be more successful when you are happy from inside, in good health, and have a level of balance in life.

If you are worried about making more and more money, accumulating more and more, and being attached to it, you will never be at peace. *If you are stressed about success all the time, losing your sleep over it, and getting frustrated over it, then you need to stop and think right now before it's too late to come out of this trap.* One day you will realize what good use it was. Let things naturally come to you after you know you have put in work.

Imagine you not being able to make wise use of the money that you accumulated. If you ignored education, relationships, health, and intellectual pursuits in a race to win, then that wealth is not going to compensate for that emptiness in your soul. *If you are poor from the soul, how can you say you are rich?* You will pay a hefty price for that.

To live a spirit-filled life in this busy, chaotic world is something you should aim for. *Your ego demands materialism, but your soul demands peace.* Your ego demands you to boast about your acquired things, but deep inside all you want is bliss. Later on in life, these acquired riches won't help you in the next realm. **The Talmud teaches the importance of not being greedy, but having sufficient wealth to survive in comfort**. Everyone's comfort level is different, that I agree on. Even in Jewish tradition, much focus is laid on savoring life by finding a middle path which will help you strike a balance among spiritual, emotional, and physical health. Moses Maimonides Ramban, a great Jewish thinker and physician, also advocated the pursuit of the middle path.

Maimonides, a Jewish philosopher, suggested that life should always be governed by the mida beinonit. Maimonides, in his *Mishneh Torah* and *Guide for the Perplexed*, discusses the concept of the mean as a key aspect of ethical behavior. He advises that virtue lies in moderation and balance. According to him, each character trait should be moderated to avoid extremes; excessive or deficient behavior leads to moral and spiritual imbalance. The concept of the *Mida Beinonit* is relevant today in various aspects of life, including work-life balance, managing stress, and ethical decision-making. It encourages individuals to find a balanced approach in all areas of life, ensuring that no single aspect dominates to the detriment of others.

When you distribute your time and energy across different aspects of life – work, health, relationships, and personal interests – you create a more balanced and rewarding existence. *As one proverb goes, "Sometimes you have to stop working and let the world catch up to you."* This highlights the value of taking time to rest and reflect, rather than constantly working.

The Tale of the Wise Old Tree

In a lush forest far away, there was a wise old tree named Eldertree. Eldertree had witnessed many seasons and had become a symbol of wisdom and balance. The animals of the forest often sought Eldertree's counsel.

One day, a young squirrel named Nutty rushed to Eldertree, panicked and exhausted. Nutty had been gathering acorns non-stop, thinking that if he stored more than any other squirrel, he would be safe through the winter. But instead of feeling secure, Nutty felt overwhelmed and unhappy.

Eldertree listened patiently and then shared his wisdom. "In our forest, every creature has its role. The bees work hard, but they also take time to enjoy the flowers. The deer run swiftly, but they rest under the shade of trees. Balance is not about working harder than others, but about ensuring that every aspect of life—work, rest, and play—is given its due."

"Nutty," Eldertree continued, "If you focus only on gathering acorns without taking time to rest or enjoy the beauty around you, you may find yourself with plenty of acorns but without the joy of living. The balance between effort and relaxation is what ensures a fulfilling life."

This story is a reminder that finding balance isn't about abandoning your passions, but integrating them with other vital aspects of life. By acknowledging and addressing the traps of overworking and rediscovering joy in other areas, you can lead a more harmonious and fulfilling life.

Reflections on Balance

1. **Work to Live, Not Live to Work:** You should remember that work is a means to support your life, not your whole life. Life is precious and meant to be relished. Work should enable you to live well, not dominate your life as I said at the beginning of chapter.

2. **Time is Limited:** Time is a finite resource, and prioritizing how you spend it is essential. Recognize that you can't do everything, and making thoughtful choices about where to invest your time can help maintain balance.

3. **Prioritizing What Matters:** Identifying and focusing on your core priorities—such as health, family, personal growth, and happiness—can help you make decisions that support a more balanced life.

4. **The Ripple Effect:** Imbalance in one area of life often affects others. For example, stress from work can impact health and relationships. Recognizing this interconnectedness can help you address imbalances holistically.

5. **Self-Compassion:** Being kind to yourself and recognizing that you can't do everything perfectly is crucial. Self-compassion allows you to approach life's challenges with a balanced perspective.

6. **Value of Rest and Recovery:** Rest is as essential as effort. Understanding that downtime and recovery are integral parts of productivity and well-being helps in maintaining a sustainable balance.

7. **The Power of Choice:** You have the power to choose how to spend your time and energy. Being intentional about these choices can help you create a balanced life that aligns with your values and goals.

Wisdom to Enlighten

FOCUS ON INCREASING SATTVA

The Concept of *Sattva*: In Hinduism, *Sattva* represents purity, harmony, and balance. The *Bhagavad Gita* (18.20) explains, "Sattva is characterized by knowledge, understanding, and joy. It leads one to a state of clarity and balance."

Maintaining the *Sattva* Guna means nurturing mental and physical health alongside pursuing one's duties. To enhance Sattva Guna, adopt a lifestyle and mindset that foster clarity, compassion, and tranquility. This involves designing your environment and daily routines to nurture positivity, purity, and peace. It will encourage you to reflect on various facets of life: mind, body, and spirit; health, wealth, and relationships; the interplay between material possessions and inner tranquility; and the importance of a balanced work-life dynamic. By harmonizing these elements, you pave the way for a richer, more meaningful life.

Sikhism

- **Balancing Work and Spirituality:** Sikh teachings emphasize the importance of living a balanced life. Guru Nanak Dev Ji said, "One who works hard and honestly, eats with contentment and shares with others, is blessed" (Guru Granth Sahib). This reflects the need to balance hard work with honest living and community sharing.

Taoism

- **Flow with Nature:** Taoist philosophy emphasizes living in harmony with the Tao (the Way). The Tao Te Ching advises, "To attain knowledge, add things every day. To attain wisdom, remove things every day" (Tao Te Ching 48). *This suggests that simplicity and balance, rather than overworking, lead to wisdom and harmony in life.* The *Tao Te Ching* also states, "Those who flow as life flows know they need no other force" (Tao Te Ching 34). This suggests that harmony with the natural flow of life, rather than exerting excessive force or effort, is key to maintaining balance in your life. Do not force things, let them be. *This perspective encourages you to trust in the natural order of things, highlighting the power of patience and surrender in achieving harmony and fulfillment.*

Judaism

- **Balance in Life:** The concept of *Shalom Bayit* **(peace in the home)** and the emphasis on rest and Sabbath reflect the importance of balance. The Talmud teaches, "One who is in good health and possesses enough food to eat, yet is not content, is considered as if he is in a state of distress" (Berakhot 60b). This suggests that physical health and emotional contentment are intertwined and essential for a balanced life.

Christianity: Rest is a blessing

Rest and Rejuvenation: In Psalm 127:2, it says, "In vain you rise early and stay up late, toiling for food to eat—for he grants sleep to those he loves." *This emphasizes that overworking and neglecting rest is futile, and that adequate rest is a blessing from God.*

The Lakota people have a rich tradition of prayer and spirituality, often expressed through ceremonies, rituals, and spoken words.

The Lakota have various prayers and teachings centered around balance and harmony, reflecting their deep connection to the natural world and spiritual principles. While there isn't a single "Lakota prayer for balance," the following is a prayer that embodies the essence of seeking balance and harmony in life.

Prayer

O Great Spirit,

Creator of the Earth and Sky, of all that is seen and unseen, I come to you with a humble heart.

Help me find balance in my life, as the sun and moon balance the day and night.

Guide me to walk the path of harmony, to be in balance with the Earth and all her creatures.

Let my actions be guided by wisdom, my heart by compassion, and my spirit by strength.

May I honor the gifts of life and the lessons they bring, living in harmony with all that surrounds me.

Help me to be at peace within myself, to balance my mind, body and spirit.

As I seek balance in my life, may I also help to bring balance to the world around me.

With gratitude and respect, I ask for your guidance.

Amen.

The Trap of not Understanding the Amazing Power of Human Mind and Thoughts

The Mindset Limitation Trap

"Master your mind with a clear sankalpa (intention), for when you control your thoughts, you control your life."

The human mind has indescribable powers, yet many fail to realize that. If your mind is at peace and free from negative notions, then your mind can totally transform and elevate you. *The human mind is an enigmatic entity, capable of both monumental creation and self-destruction.* Its potential is vast, yet it remains largely untapped by many. Central to this untapped potential is the state of mental tranquility. *When the mind is liberated from the constraints of negativity and internal turmoil, it becomes a formidable tool for your personal transformation and elevation.* Understanding how peace of mind fosters this transformation requires a deep dive into the interplay between mental serenity, cognitive function, and personal growth.

You can manifest your deepest desires or undergo personal transformation through mental clarity. *Your mind and, essentially, your thoughts have the power to shape who you are and who you want to become.* We all have a strong desire to live our life well by living to our truest potential and achieve the best of things. How you become and what you make out of your life all depends on your thoughts. *Yet we fall into the trap of believing that someone else is responsible for our misery or problems.* We keep thinking that someone will take us out from the clutches of life's problems. But it is your own mind that can help you if you make it your friend. You have the potential to overcome anything in this world. You have the power within you to fulfill your truest desires if you have a peaceful, controlled mind and powerful, healthy thoughts devoid of toxic patterns of thinking.

The Nature of a Peaceful Mind

A peaceful mind is characterized by an absence of disruptive thoughts, emotional turbulence, and self-limiting beliefs. *It is a state of equilibrium where the individual is not dominated by anxiety, fear, or doubt.* Instead, it is marked by clarity, focus, and a balanced emotional state. This mental clarity is not merely a transient experience but a stable condition that can significantly influence how one perceives and interacts with the world.

If you are going through an emotional turbulence, you will witness that it clouds your judgment and impairs decision-making. *A peaceful mind enhances emotional regulation; you have the right thoughts leading to more rational and balanced responses to challenges faced by you.* This improved emotional resilience not only helps you in managing stress but also in maintaining a balanced outlook. **Only in a peaceful mind dwells its true purpose.**

In Hinduism, the Vedas have also recognized the manifesting powers of the mind. They have eulogized the mind as the Brahman or Creator himself. If the mind is filled with Sattva Guna, or pure thoughts, then it is able to achieve the highest wisdom and becomes a magnet to attract all good things in life.

In Hinduism and the Puranas, the power of the mind and thoughts is deeply acknowledged as a fundamental force in shaping one's destiny and achieving spiritual goals. **The concepts of Sankalpa, Chitta, Karma, and Siddhi illustrate to us the significant role of mental focus and intention in the manifestation process.** One of the key concepts is **"Sankalpa"**, the power of intention. According to Hindu beliefs, Sankalpa, when combined with devotion and disciplined action, has the power to manifest desires. It is a heartfelt resolution or intention, a conscious choice that aligns one's thoughts and actions with their true purpose. It helps in focusing your scattered mind on one resolution and keeping it stable. Sankalpa can lead to significant internal changes. *When you hold a strong resolve, it can shift your mindset, enhance your self-discipline, and foster personal growth.* These internal transformations can manifest as external changes in your life.

Sankalpa channels your mental and emotional energy toward a specific objective. This focused energy helps you overcome obstacles, stay motivated, and take consistent actions that are aligned with your goal. Suppose your mind is always more interested in what others are doing than in doing what you need to do. It will create feelings of jealousy, greed, competitiveness, or complexes, whether inferiority or superiority. Such feelings lead you to take useless actions, creating unnecessary karma. This, in turn, pollutes the mind, adds confusion, leading to futile actions and causing you to miss your goal. *A polluted & confused mind can never reach its truest potential or keep up with a resolve.* To clear confusion, you have to build your sankalpa shakti. Your intentions and thoughts guide your actions. Positive thoughts and intentions can lead to positive actions and outcomes, while negative thoughts and intentions can lead to less favorable results.

Think of **sankalpa** as a powerful **arrow**. Here's an analogy to illustrate its impact:

The Arrow of Sankalpa

1. **Drawing the Bow (Formulating the Sankalpa)**: Imagine you are an archer, and your sankalpa is the arrow you're preparing to shoot. The process of drawing the bow represents the careful formulation of your intention. Just as an archer must carefully aim and draw the bow to ensure accuracy, you must clearly define and focus your sankalpa.

2. **The Pull of the Bowstring (Commitment and Focus)**: As you pull the bowstring back, you are investing your energy, concentration, and commitment into the arrow. This act of pulling represents the power and resolve you put into your sankalpa. The stronger the pull, the more potential energy the arrow will have.

3. **Releasing the Arrow (Acting on the Sankalpa)**: When you release the arrow, it flies toward its target with the force generated by your effort.

This is akin to taking actions that align with your sankalpa. The arrow's trajectory is influenced by how well you've aimed and the strength of your pull, similar to how your actions are influenced by the clarity and intensity of your intention.

4. **Hitting the Target (Manifesting the Intention)**: If the arrow is well-aimed and released with sufficient force, it hits the target accurately. This represents the manifestation of your sankalpa. Just as a well-shot arrow can reach and impact its target, a powerful sankalpa can guide your actions and circumstances to align with your intended outcome.

5. **Changing the Course (Transforming Destiny)**: Just as the arrow, once released, can alter the path of its journey, a strong sankalpa can significantly change the course of your life. **The impact of the arrow hitting the target can be likened to how a well-formulated intention can influence and reshape your destiny.**

Thereby, your sankalpa is like an arrow: the more focused and powerful your intention, the more effectively it can steer the course of your life toward your desired outcome. Just as an archer's skill and intention shape the flight of the arrow, your resolve and actions shape the trajectory of your destiny.

Thoughts and Right energy

Therefore, it can be deduced that the power lies in your thoughts. Thoughts are built on the way you think, and these become substances in your brain which feed it, and accordingly, your actions are guided by it. Mere thoughts won't do much until and unless you empower those thoughts with the right energy. So, with every beautiful and noble thought, a beautiful action takes place. With a very powerful thought, a dynamic action takes place.

Now, what you add to this powerful thought is what determines the ultimate outcome.

Powerful thought + Right intention + Positive vibrations = Positive dynamic action or outcome

Powerful thought + Malevolent intention + Negative vibrations = Negative outcome

Your intentions and the frequency you are vibrating will dictate the outcome of your actions. If your thought is created in a powerful way, without any negative thoughts bringing down the intensity of the thought process, it will manifest.

Come Out of the Trap of an Impure Mind

The purified mind has all the powers of Iccha (willpower), **Gyana shakti** (knowledge to discern), and Kriya, which are like supreme powers. When the mind is purified, you gain greater self-awareness, recognizing your strengths, weaknesses, and true desires. A pure mind is characterized by clarity, emotional stability, wisdom, positive intentions, and discipline, leading to a harmonious and productive life. In contrast, an impure mind is often marked by clutter, emotional turmoil, lack of insight, self-centeredness, and impulsivity, which can hinder personal growth and well-being.

Imagine you are wearing a pair of clear, clean glasses. Through these glasses, you see the world clearly, with no distortions or obstructions. Your perception is accurate, and you can easily navigate and understand your surroundings. Now, imagine wearing glasses that are smudged, dirty, or foggy. Your vision is blurred, and it's difficult to see things clearly. Your understanding of the world is clouded by these impurities, leading to confusion and misinterpretation. Therefore, with a pure mind, one gains deeper understanding and insight. There is a capacity to discern truth from falsehood and to make decisions based on wisdom rather than impulse.

Lord Krishna tells Arjuna that, *"One must deliver himself with the help of his mind, and not degrade himself. The mind is the friend of the conditioned soul, and his enemy as well"* (Bhagavad Gita 6.5). And *"For him who has conquered the mind, the mind is the best of friends; but for one who has failed to do so, his mind will remain the greatest enemy"* (Bhagavad Gita 6.6).

You will live like a king if you master the art of controlling the mind and not as a slave of the mind. You will be able to enjoy every moment of your life based on the power of your mind. The mind is the most precious gift to you by the Divine.

It is a source of creativity, self-discovery, and transformation. Recognizing its value will encourage practices that enhance mental clarity, emotional stability, and spiritual growth, reflecting its sacred and profound nature to you. By appreciating and nurturing this gift, you can align with your highest potential, and this will contribute meaningfully to your life and the world.

Exercise: Harnessing the Power of Mind through Thoughts and Sankalpa

Mindfulness Meditation (10 minutes)

1. **Focus on Your Breath**: Inhale deeply through your nose, allowing your belly to rise. Exhale slowly through your mouth, letting go of any tension. Continue this for a few minutes to calm your mind.

2. **Observe Your Thoughts**: Simply notice any thoughts that arise without judgment. Let them come and go, bringing your focus back to your breath if you get distracted.

Define Your Sankalpa (10 minutes)

1. **Reflect on Your Intention**: Think about a specific goal or change you want to achieve. It should be something meaningful and aligned with your values.

2. **Craft Your Sankalpa**: Write down your intention in a positive and present-tense statement. For example, "I am confidently achieving my goals," or "I am embracing peace and calm in my daily life."

   Practice: Integrate your sankalpa into your health routines. For example, if your sankalpa is about vitality, set intentions to eat nutritious meals, exercise regularly, and get adequate rest.

   Mindful Leisure:

   Practice: Engage in leisure activities with a mindful intention. For example, if your sankalpa involves relaxation, approach activities like reading or hobbies with full presence and enjoyment.

Set Daily Goals:

Practice: Define specific, actionable goals that align with your sankalpa. For example, if your sankalpa is to improve productivity, set goals like completing key tasks or managing time effectively. Maintain a diary for this.

It totally depends on your goals. Craft your goal.

3. **Repetition and Visualization:** Read your sankalpa aloud, and visualize yourself living it out. Imagine the feelings, experiences, and outcomes associated with your intention.

Affirmation and Reinforcement (10 minutes)

1. **Develop Affirmations**:

    o   **Practice**: Write a few affirmations that reinforce your sankalpa. For instance, "I am resilient and adaptable," or "Every day, I am making progress toward my new beginning."

    o   **Purpose**: Affirmations help in maintaining a positive mindset and reinforce your sankalpa.

2. **Repeat Affirmations**:

    o   **Practice**: Recite these affirmations daily, either in the morning or before bed. Feel the truth and emotion behind each affirmation.

    o   **Purpose**: Regular repetition helps embed your sankalpa into your subconscious mind.

The Trap of not Taking Charge of Your Feelings or Emotions After Going Through a Bad Experience or Sadness

The Emotional Entanglement Trap

"You may not control all the events that happen to you,
but you can decide not to be reduced by them."
- Maya Angelou

"Let all experiences touch you—both the bliss and the hardship. Keep going, for every emotion is temporary."

In life, you should be able to control your emotions rather than emotions taking control over you. Do not let the negative emotions related to bad or rough experiences darken your soul. You can't choose to numb your emotions selectively. If you numb the dark, then you numb the light. Light only enters when you recognize that there is darkness that needs to go. **If you suppress the darkness, you also block the light. True illumination comes when you acknowledge the shadows and allow them to fade.** Darkness should not engulf you; rather, it should illuminate the path to growth and resilience.

In life bad experiences can have a profound impact on your emotional and mental well-being, and if not managed properly, they can indeed cast a shadow over your inner life.

You lose your true identity and the beautiful being that you were all the time. *It can challenge or shatter one's sense of identity.* For instance, a sudden career setback or personal failure might make someone question their self-worth or purpose in life. Often, people fall into the trap of not taking charge of their feelings, resulting in a cynical outlook on life and relationships, making it hard to experience joy or connect with others meaningfully. They become miserable later in life dealing with the identity crisis of not knowing who they truly are and what they want from life. Was their life worthwhile? Was there anything that stopped them from gaining control over their life? What were their lessons? Were their emotions too dominant to let them make the right choices in life? All these questions haunt them.

I am sure you would agree on this - Emotions or feelings, if left unchecked, can be a cause of turmoil in your life. Emotions are like weather – sunny, bright, stormy, cloudy, or tempestuous. Like weather keeps on changing, your emotions also go through changes. You should know the weather inside you to let it pass over time. *You can only take charge of your feelings when you are aware of what is going inside you. It is not about being devoid of emotions but is about experiencing them without attachment and identification and being able to take charge of them.* Since emotions are springs of action which can largely determine the quality of your life and your interactions with people around you. Your actions are often a direct response to your emotional state. Emotions greatly affect how you interact with others. Positive emotions like empathy and love can strengthen relationships, while negative emotions like anger, insecurity, or resentment can create conflicts. Emotional intelligence helps navigate and enhance these interactions. It has a direct impact on your behavior too. For example, feeling stressed might lead someone to seek comfort through food or withdraw from social interactions. Conversely, feeling fulfilled might inspire someone to engage in productive or creative activities.

How Emotions act as a Fuel to your actions

- **Positive Emotions**: Imagine filling your vehicle with high-quality, clean fuel. This type of fuel allows your vehicle to run smoothly, accelerate efficiently, and reach its destination with fewer problems. Positive emotions like joy, enthusiasm, and love provide a sense of motivation and drive, helping you navigate life's challenges effectively and pursue goals with vigor.

- **Negative Emotions**: Now, consider using low-quality or contaminated fuel. This can cause the vehicle to sputter, lose power, or even break down. Negative emotions, such as anger, fear, or sadness, can similarly impair your ability to act effectively, leading to obstacles in achieving your goals and affecting overall well-being. They can leave you feeling stuck and drained, casting a shadow over your energy and mindset.

All your actions are guided by your emotional experiences from the past and the current state of emotions. Take charge of your feelings and do not keep them repressed. *Emotional disturbances need to be dealt with and healed. If you are sad, do not repress that sadness; feel it in every way. Go right through that state of sadness, grief, but emerge out stronger as a wiser and better person.*

Ask yourself what is it that is making you sad?

- Is it too much attachment? Do you have an unhealthy dependency on relationships or possessions?

- Is it the fear of missing out on something?

- Is it the need to possess something?

- Is it the fear of facing your fears?

- Is it the behavior of a close one affecting you? If their behavior is hurtful or disruptive?

- Is it the hurt from your past? (Emotional hurt from past experiences, relationships, or personal failures can linger and cause sadness. This hurt might stem from unresolved issues or trauma).

If you keep repressing the feeling of sadness or any uncomfortable feeling inside you, you will be in misery. Accumulation of negative emotions can lead to stress, anxiety, or depression. Such emotions are like wounds; if left untreated, they can become infected. You need to heal them by addressing them. Healing involves acknowledging the pain, understanding its source, and taking steps to address and resolve it. Do not avoid them; rather address them. *If you are not sensitive to your emotions, you aren't sensitive to others as well.* There is a disconnect. That sadness needs to be addressed and coped with to reach the neutral stage and then to a stage where you are empowered enough to overcome it.

Stoics recognize that while we cannot control the occurrence of sadness, we can control our response to it. Accepting sadness as a natural part of life, rather than resisting or repressing it, aligns with the Stoic practice of accepting what is beyond our control. By fully experiencing and reflecting on sadness, you gain wisdom and develop virtue. The Stoic approach involves observing your emotional responses with equanimity, learning from them, and using this understanding to cultivate inner peace and resilience. True happiness and fulfillment come from living a life of virtue rather than from external circumstances. *By focusing on virtues such as wisdom, courage, justice, and temperance, you can find stability and contentment even in the face of sadness.*

Practical Application of Virtues

WISDOM TO HELP YOU COME OUT OF THE TRAP

- **Reflect on the Nature of Sadness**: Use wisdom to understand that sadness is temporary and part of the broader human experience. Everyone goes through these emotions. None is spared. Marcus Aurelius views suffering and sadness as part of the broader human experience. He emphasizes that these feelings are natural and should be accepted as such, rather than seen as personal failures or injustices. Reflect on your past experiences where you overcame similar feelings and use that knowledge to navigate your current situation. Place your suffering in a larger context, think about the countless people who have faced similar struggles throughout history can help to diminish the sense of isolation or uniqueness in one's own suffering.

- **Seek Knowledge**: You should read philosophical texts, engage in introspective practices, or seek guidance from mentors to gain a deeper understanding of how to handle emotions effectively. Knowledge and self-awareness will equip you with the tools to understand and manage your emotions, helping you sail through life's challenges with clarity and resilience.

Courage

- **Face Your Emotions**: Allow yourself to feel and acknowledge sadness without avoidance. Use courage to confront the source of your sadness and address it directly. If your sadness is related to interpersonal issues, approach conversations with those involved with honesty and bravery. Express your feelings and concerns directly, while also being open to listening and understanding their perspective. Never lose hope and courage. Let them be your guiding light.

Philosophical Views

- **Epictetus**, a Stoic philosopher, said: *"It's not what happens to you, but how you react to it that matters."* This quote emphasizes that while you may not be able to control the source of your sadness, you definitely have the power to respond to it with courage and intention. Your reaction—whether you choose to face the issue head-on or avoid it—determines how you navigate and ultimately overcome your emotional challenges.

- **Marcus Aurelius**: "The impediment to action advances action. What stands in the way becomes the way." This quote gives you the wisdom that challenges and sources of sadness can be transformed into opportunities for growth and action if approached with courage.

- **Pema Chödrön**: "The only way to deal with our pain is to lean into it, to touch it and go through it rather than trying to avoid it." Pema Chödrön advocates for embracing and facing our emotional pain directly, including sadness, as a path to healing and understanding.

- **Take Action**: Even when feeling sad, continue to engage in activities that align with your values and goals. Courage allows you to act in spite of emotional discomfort. It is the antidote to sadness, giving you the strength to move forward, even when the weight of emotions threatens to hold you back.

- **Justice**: Be fair to yourself while empathizing with others.

- **Be Fair to Yourself**: Recognize your own needs and limitations during times of sadness. Avoid being overly harsh or critical of yourself and instead practice self-compassion. *Whenever you catch yourself being self-critical, question those thoughts.* Ask yourself whether you would say the same things to someone you care about. Often, we are much harsher with ourselves than with others. You can transform self-critical thoughts into more supportive and constructive ones. **For example, instead of thinking, "I'm failing at handling this," reframe it to, "I'm doing the best I can in a difficult situation."** Keep talking to yourself like you would to someone you love when they are facing tough times. Keep doing this until you are yourself again. **Remind yourself it's okay; things happen, people change, but life goes on.**

- **Empathize with Others**: Apply justice by understanding and empathizing with the feelings of others who may be experiencing their own challenges. This fosters mutual support and strengthens relationships.

Virtue of Temperance

- **Manage Your Reactions**: You should practice moderation in how you respond to sadness. Avoid excessive indulgence in self-pity or escapism, and instead find a balanced approach to managing your emotions. If we talk about Sufism, **Tazkiyah** is the process of purifying the soul. It is purifying the soul or self from impurities and vices, leading to spiritual clarity and closeness to God. *Sadness can be a catalyst for this inner purification, leading to spiritual rebirth and greater alignment with divine will.* Feeling sad often leads us to reflect on our lives and relationships, prompting introspection and a search for deeper meaning. In these moments, sadness serves as a messenger, helping us identify what's wrong and guiding us toward necessary changes. *Isn't it beautiful?*

- **Set Healthy Boundaries**: Use temperance to set boundaries that help maintain emotional stability, such as balancing time spent on introspection with time spent engaging in positive activities. *Do what you love and go into a shell to find the center.*

Wisdom from Sufism: Some Sufi practices to deal with Sadness

Meditation and Contemplation

- Engaging in meditation and contemplation helps deepen one's awareness of the Divine presence and find inner peace amid sadness.

  "In the silence of meditation, the heart finds its true voice."

Spiritual Retreats (Khalwa)

- **Khalwa** or spiritual retreat involves isolating oneself for a period to focus on prayer, reflection, and spiritual growth. This practice can provide a renewed perspective and relief from emotional turmoil. It works wonders! Trust me.

  "In solitude, the soul's whispers become clearer."

Gratitude Practice (Shukr)

- **Shukr** or gratitude is a fundamental aspect of Sufi practice. Cultivating gratitude for the blessings in one's life, even during times of sadness, can shift focus and bring a sense of peace.

  "Gratitude turns what we have into enough."

Turning Sadness into Praise of God: Divert your attention to something meaningful

- Transforming sadness into a form of **Dhikr** or remembrance, turning grief into praise, can be a powerful way to transcend the pain and connect with the Divine.

  "Let your tears become prayers, and your heart will be healed."

Seeking Divine Mercy (Rahma)

- **Rahma** It is derived from the Arabic word "rahmah," which translates to "mercy" or "compassion")refers to divine mercy and compassion. Sufis seek to invoke and experience this mercy in their lives, finding solace and healing through the Divine's boundless compassion.

"The Divine mercy embraces all. In it, every heart finds peace." (Anonymous Sufi)

To overcome the trap of not taking charge of your feelings after a difficult experience or sadness, **it is crucial to actively engage with your emotions.** Later in life, many people come to regret not taking charge of their emotions and feelings after experiencing sadness or difficult times, which led to prolonged suffering, missed opportunities for growth, and unresolved issues that impact their overall well-being. *Later in life, this lack of emotional management can result in deep-seated regret, as they realize that confronting and dealing with their feelings sooner could have led to a healthier, more fulfilling life.* Taking proactive steps in coming out of this trap by addressing and managing emotions early on is thereby crucial for preventing these regrets and fostering long-term emotional resilience and growth.

Pearls of Wisdom

Suffering or *dukha* arises from within and not from the outside world. *Bhagavad Gita* traces all emotional experiences to the *gunas, i.e., sattva, rajas, and tamas.*

Cheerfulness, joy, bliss, forgiveness, and equanimity are associated with *sattva. Rajas* gives rise to discontent, mental agony, grief, greed, hatred, and intolerance. Fatigue, "delusion," indolence, and non-discrimination (between the pleasant and the good) are due to *tamas*. Hence, it is suggested that men should strive to increase the *sattvic guna.*

If we understand it in the modern concept, it guides us to move toward positive emotions and increase more of it. Release what no longer serves you. Each layer of negativity you shed makes room for light, kindness, and joy, which are the essence of *sattva.*

"Like the rising sun dispelling the darkness, the light of *sattva* grows as we nurture simplicity, contentment, and inner clarity, allowing our true nature to shine through."

The Trap of Being Too Helpful: Navigating the Balance Between Support and Self-Care

The Altruism Trap

"Generosity without boundaries is a well that runs dry. Tend to your own heart, so that you may continue to nourish others with true wisdom."

In a world that values kindness and altruism, it's easy to fall into the trap of being too helpful by being naive. *The desire to assist others can be commendable, but when taken to extremes, it can lead to personal burnout and unbalanced relationships.* Understanding the boundaries of helpfulness and learning to navigate this balance is crucial for maintaining both your well-being and effective support for others. Sometimes, by helping others too much, you end up hurting yourself. In a world that often celebrates selflessness and generosity, the notion of "stop helping everyone" might seem counterintuitive or even harsh. However, it's crucial to understand that helping others, while valuable, should be balanced with self-care and boundaries. Overextending yourself to meet everyone's needs can lead to burnout, diminished effectiveness, and strained relationships.

Sometimes you might be a person of good heart, but another person might be using you for their selfish motives or to build their own goodwill by being in association with you as you have that goodwill. Someone would want to be associated with you to learn something from you or gain something out of you. There are also people who would give their life to save someone, but then the other person would turn up and say, "Did I ask you to?" Not a very pleasant thing to hear. Right? The time that you devote to helping others by overextending yourself could be spent on you and your well-being. You could utilize that time to make something for yourself, however small it is. Not everyone deserves your kindness. *There are worthy people who deserve your help, but then there can be selfish people too.* Before helping people, you need to assess that helping them should not cost your peace, time, and energy. More than anything, it should not cost your emotions. **Save your heart by avoiding helping people who are mean and change with time and situations.** Protect your heart from those who wear kindness as a mask, only to reveal cruelty when circumstances shift. Some people change with time, but their disregard for your soul remains the same. Don't give your love to those who will only take it and leave you empty.

There are people who will talk to you or seek your support when they need something from you. It's a common experience to encounter individuals who reach out for support only when they need something from you, whether it's advice, assistance, or emotional support.

"Beware of those who seek your help only when they have a need, yet vanish when you require the same in return. True connections are built on mutual support, not one-sided dependence. Recognize those who take without giving, and protect your energy from those who only come when it serves them."

While it's natural to want to be helpful and supportive, it's important to navigate these relationships with awareness and balance. Here's how to recognize and manage these one-sided dynamics effectively.

Understanding One-Sided Relationships

In relationships where support is sought only when it benefits the other person and there's little to no reciprocation, it's easy to feel used or undervalued. These one-sided interactions can drain your energy and diminish your sense of fulfillment. It's important to recognize when it's appropriate to step back and prioritize your own well-being. Here is how you can identify them.

1. **Transactional Interactions**: In one-sided relationships, the interaction often feels transactional; people reach out primarily when they need something, rather than engaging in a mutually supportive and reciprocal relationship. Such connections are driven by selfishness, leaving you feeling used and drained, rather than valued and respected.

2. **Lack of Engagement**: When these individuals only contact you during their times of need, it can create a sense of imbalance, as there is minimal engagement or connection during times when they don't require assistance.

3. **Emotional Toll**: Constantly being approached only when someone needs something can be emotionally draining for you. It may leave you feeling used or undervalued, especially if there is no reciprocal support or acknowledgment later.

Recognizing the Signs

1. **Infrequent Communication**: They rarely communicate or interact with you unless they need something. Their contact is sporadic and often driven by their immediate needs.

2. **Minimal Acknowledgment**: They may show little appreciation or acknowledgment for the support you provide, which can leave you feeling unappreciated.

3. **Unbalanced Reciprocity**: The relationship feels unbalanced, with a significant disparity between the help you offer and the support or engagement you receive in return.

4. **High Dependency**: They may demonstrate a pattern of high dependency on your assistance, without showing initiative to solve their own problems or seek solutions independently.

Strategies for Managing One-Sided Relationships

1. **Set Clear Boundaries**: Establish and communicate clear boundaries regarding the extent of support you are willing to offer. It's important to protect your own well-being and prevent overextending yourself.

2. **Assess Your Own Needs**: Reflect on how these interactions affect you emotionally and mentally. Consider whether the relationship aligns with your values and if it meets your own needs for connection and reciprocity or not.

3. **Encourage Independence**: When offering support, aim to empower the individual to find their own solutions. Encourage them to seek resources or take steps toward resolving their issues independently.

4. **Communicate Expectations**: If you feel comfortable, address the issue directly. Let the person know how their behavior affects you and discuss ways to create a more balanced and mutually supportive relationship.

5. **Limit Availability**: *You have the right to limit your availability if you feel that the relationship is consistently one-sided.* Prioritize your own needs and well-being over constantly being available to others.

6. **Seek Reciprocity**: Foster relationships where there is mutual support and respect. *Surround yourself with people who contribute positively to your life and where there is a balance of giving and receiving.* Invest your time and energy in relationships where there is mutual support and respect. Surround yourself with people who appreciate and reciprocate your efforts.

7. **Practice Self-Care**: Protect your own emotional health by engaging in self-care practices. Ensure that you have time and space to recharge and maintain your own well-being.

Strategies for Balanced Helping

- **Reflect on Motivations**: Regularly assess your motivations for helping. Ensure that your desire to assist others aligns with your own values and goals, rather than stemming from a need to gain approval or avoid conflict.

- **Seek Support**: Just as you offer support to others, seek support for yourself when needed. Whether through friends, family, or professional help, having a support network can provide you with the resources to maintain balance.

- **Practice Mindfulness**: Mindfulness techniques can help you stay present and aware of your own needs and boundaries. Being mindful can assist in recognizing when you're overcommitting and need to recalibrate.

Story of The Overburdened Gardener

In the heart of a bustling town, there was a gardener named Dia. Her garden was renowned for its vibrant blooms and lush greenery, and she took great pride in her work. Known for her generosity, Dia was always ready to help her neighbors with their own gardens, offering advice, weeding, and watering whenever needed.

One summer, the town's garden fair approached, and Dia was excited to showcase her beautiful garden. However, as the fair drew closer, Dia's neighbors began asking for more help than usual. They needed assistance with pest control, pruning, and even last-minute plantings. Dia, eager to help, devoted all her time to their requests.

As the days passed, Dia's own garden was neglected. Weeds began to overrun her flower beds, and the once-healthy plants started to droop. By the day of the fair, her garden looked unkempt compared to its usual splendor.

The fair began, and Dia walked through the garden exhibits with a heavy heart. Her neighbors' gardens were flourishing, but hers was barely recognizable. As the judges made their rounds, Dia felt a pang of regret.

Seeing her distress, the town's wise old gardener, Mr. Freddy, approached her. "Dia," he said gently, "you've helped everyone so much, but what about your own garden?"

She sighed, "I wanted to help, but I ended up neglecting my own."

Mr. Freddy nodded understandingly. *"Helping others is a noble thing, but not at the expense of your own well-being. Balance is key. Make sure to tend to your own garden before extending yourself too thin."*

Dia took his words to heart. Over the next few weeks, she focused on restoring her garden, slowly but surely bringing it back to its former glory. She continued to help her neighbors, but with a newfound balance, ensuring her own garden thrived as well.

By the next fair, Dia's garden was once again the pride of the town. Her experience had taught her a valuable lesson: while helping others was important, maintaining her own well-being was equally crucial.

The Spiritual Perspective on Being Too Helping

- In the realm of spiritual growth and wisdom, the concept of being overly helpful touches on deeper themes of balance, self-care, and the nature of true service. **From a spiritual perspective, the act of giving should be an expression of one's inner abundance, rather than a source of depletion or sacrifice.**

- Spiritual teachings often highlight the law of reciprocity, which suggests that what we give will eventually return to us in some form. When we give too much and neglect our own needs, we might find ourselves feeling unappreciated or drained. This imbalance can hinder the natural flow of energy and create blockages in receiving the support and love we also deserve. *By maintaining a healthy balance in giving and receiving, we ensure that our interactions are harmonious and that the flow of energy is mutual.* This not only supports our spiritual growth but also enhances our ability to engage with others in a meaningful and constructive way.

"Embody the law of reciprocity: our gifts to the world ultimately return to us. By cultivating a balanced exchange between giving and receiving, we foster harmonious connections that not only nourish our spiritual evolution but also elevate the quality of our engagements with others."

The Trap of not Embracing Simplicity and Finding Beauty in Simple Things

The Essence Overlook Trap

"Simplicity is not about settling for less, but about recognizing the richness in what is often overlooked. True fulfillment comes from appreciating the simple, meaningful things."

Life does not have to be extravagant to be exciting. Most people are trying to find happiness in things that are shallow and pretentious. We have stopped looking for happiness in simple things. *Embracing simplicity doesn't mean you become complacent or less competitive.* It is good to be ambitious, to have goals in life and be a driven person. Your passion should drive you, motivate you to achieve finer things but never stop finding joy in simpler things in life. *When you embrace simplicity, you tend to uncomplicate your life and focus on things that really matter.* You start working from outside in. You start removing the layers and connect with the essence. Simple things possess their own unique allure through their familiarity and unpretentious nature. It's in the everyday moments—the warmth of a cup of coffee, the rhythm of a morning rain, or the quiet comfort of a cozy blanket—that we often find the most genuine beauty.

If you really think deeply, simplicity is not about sacrificing; it is essentially a way to figure out how simple things can give you happiness and contentment. You will understand what really matters. *It opens up a space in our life where you can go out and be your authentic self, enjoy your liveliness and be with the rhythm of life.* You are free in this space with no entanglement of wants and desires. ***Desires that are influenced by others, they do not belong to us.*** You desire something because you have seen somebody with a thing (a material possession) or achieving something and you perceive and correlate their happiness with that thing. It creates a desire in you to have a similar thing so that it can make you happy, which is a false perception. Even your desire doesn't come from your core, it is largely influenced by what you see and perceive. *You lose simplicity the moment you try to become someone or copy someone mindlessly.* Try to find and give meaning to your life by simplifying it. Your time is limited so focus on what is important. Stop running after what is unnecessary; for this, you have to declutter your life. To declutter, you have to identify what is not serving any purpose, what is not adding value, what is not adding richness to your life, what is absolutely unnecessary and can be discarded.

- Do you have more free time?

- Do you spend time with your loved ones?

- Do you understand their emotional state?

- Do you set aside time for yourself? A few moments with yourself in silence and absolute peace?

- Do you enjoy the beauty of nature and soak in all the little wonderful things? Do you enjoy your food… the flavors of the food… the food for which the whole life hustle is going?

Finding beauty in simple things is about appreciating the elegance and significance in the everyday and the unadorned. Here are some ways to think about it:

1. **A Flickering Candle Flame**: It's like watching a single candle flame dance in the dark. The simplicity of its light creates a warm, calming ambiance, revealing a quiet beauty that often goes unnoticed in our busy lives. A candle's aroma, whether it's the soft scent of vanilla, the earthy notes of sandalwood, or the fresh hint of lavender, gently invites you into a moment of calm. Its simplicity lies in how a single scent can evoke memories, soothe the mind, or create a sense of warmth and comfort without overwhelming the senses.

2. **Freshly Fallen Snow**: In its pristine state, snow reminds us of the beauty in simplicity and the peace that can be found in nature's quiet moments. The pristine, unblemished white surface transforms ordinary scenes into a serene and magical wonderland, highlighting how simplicity can evoke profound beauty.

3. **A Child's Laughter**: Finding beauty in simple things is like hearing a child's genuine, unfiltered laughter. *It's pure and spontaneous, reflecting joy and innocence that remind us of the simple pleasures in life.* A child's laughter has a way of capturing the essence of life's beauty in its most unfiltered form. The sound of a child's laughter is often spontaneous and infectious, bubbling up from a place of genuine delight and wonder. It fills your soul with love and innocence.

4. **A Home-Cooked Meal**: The beauty of a home-cooked meal is found in the effort and love that goes into it. Whether it's the comforting aroma wafting through the kitchen, the sight of a dish coming together, or the shared experience of a meal, there's a warmth and authenticity that pre-packaged or restaurant food can't quite replicate. The process of cooking and sharing a meal fosters a sense of connection and care, transforming the act of eating into a meaningful experience.

5. **The Rhythm of Breathing**: *Finding beauty in simple things is like being aware of the steady rhythm of your own breath.* It's a fundamental, often overlooked part of life that underscores the beauty of existence and mindfulness.

6. **The Sound of Rain**: The sound of rain is a deeply soothing and beautiful phenomenon that speaks to the soul in a unique way. It has a way of transforming the environment, evoking a sense of calm, and inviting reflection. It's like listening to the sound of rain tapping on your window. The gentle, repetitive pattern creates a soothing, tranquil atmosphere, showing how the simplest sounds can be deeply comforting and beautiful. *Rain is a reminder of the cyclical nature of life and the essential role it plays in our ecosystem.* It reminds us that every ending carries the seed of a new beginning, nourishing not only the earth but also our spirits, reminding us that growth often comes through gentle moments of replenishment. It refreshes and nourishes the earth, symbolizing renewal and growth.

Listening to the rain can deepen our connection to the natural world and remind us of the beauty in its rhythms and processes.

In essence, finding beauty in simple things is about recognizing the value and charm in the ordinary, appreciating how these elements contribute to the richness of life.

How Can You Start to Enjoy Simple Things

1. **Slow Down and Savor**: You should take time to fully engage with and enjoy small moments. Savor a meal without rushing through the meal, linger over a conversation by showing genuine interest and empathy, or relish a quiet moment. Allow yourself to simply be without any pressure to do or achieve anything. Embrace the peace that comes with quiet. By slowing down, you give yourself the chance to experience the richness of these simple pleasures.

2. **Capture Moments**: Use a journal, camera, or smartphone to document the small, beautiful moments in your life. Create themed photo albums, such as "Scenes of Joy" or "Everyday Beauty." This can help you focus on and appreciate different aspects of your life. Sometimes, looking back at these snapshots can reveal how many simple, joyful experiences you've encountered.

3. **Embrace Minimalism**: Simplify your surroundings by decluttering and focusing on what truly matters to you. A minimalist space can enhance your ability to concentrate and feel more organized, leading to increased productivity and well-being. You may start by evaluating your possessions. Ask yourself if each item serves a purpose, brings you joy, or holds significant value. Let go of things that no longer fit these criteria. Start tackling one space at a time—such as a closet, drawer, or room—to make the decluttering process manageable and less overwhelming. Embracing minimalism involves more than just decluttering; it's about creating a space that reflects and supports your values and priorities. By focusing on what truly matters and appreciating the beauty of simplicity, you can cultivate a more meaningful and fulfilling life.

4. **Practice Mindful Eating**: Mindful eating transforms a simple meal into a symphony of senses, where each bite becomes a moment of discovery and appreciation. Pay attention to the flavors, textures, and aromas of your food. Eating mindfully can turn a simple meal into a sensory experience, enhancing your appreciation of the food and the act of eating. Arrange your meal thoughtfully, using attractive plates and utensils. Taking a moment to appreciate the presentation can enhance your enjoyment.

5. **Celebrate Small Achievements**: Recognize and celebrate your small successes and milestones. Whether it's completing a project, learning something new, or achieving a personal goal, these moments of progress are worth appreciating. Share your achievements with friends, family, or colleagues, and involve them in your celebrations when appropriate. Their support and encouragement can amplify the joy of your accomplishments. Treat yourself to a small reward, such as a favorite treat or a relaxing activity, to reinforce your success. Establish a personal ritual for celebrating milestones, and use visual tools like progress charts or checklists to track and display your progress. Practice self-compassion by being kind to yourself and acknowledging your efforts without self-criticism.By regularly celebrating these small victories, you build momentum, reinforce positive behaviors, and create a supportive environment that motivates and energizes you for future endeavors.

6. **Engage with Art**: Engaging with art, whether through creation or appreciation, transforms the ordinary into the extraordinary, filling each moment with joy and a sense of accomplishment. Create or enjoy simple forms of art, such as doodling, painting, or crafting. The act of creating or appreciating art, no matter how simple, can bring joy and a sense of accomplishment. It is magical.

7. **Connect with Your Surroundings**: Spend time in your local environment, whether it's a park, garden, or even a neighborhood street. Observing local wildlife, plants, and landscapes can reveal the unique beauty of your everyday surroundings.

8. **Practice Presence**: Focus on being fully present in each moment. When you engage with your current experience without distraction, you're more likely to notice and appreciate the small, beautiful details around you.

9. **Cultivate Relationships**: Invest time in building and nurturing relationships. Simple acts of kindness, meaningful conversations, being part of online communities with like-minded people and spending time with loved ones can highlight the beauty in human connections.

10. **Engage the Senses**: Pay attention to sensory experiences: soft textures, pleasant scents, soothing sounds, or delightful tastes. Engaging your senses can deepen your appreciation for simple pleasures.

11. **Find Joy in Routine**: Turn daily tasks into moments of joy. For example, the ritual of making your bed each morning or the satisfaction of organizing a space can become opportunities to find beauty and order in your day.

12. **Explore New Perspectives**: Change your perspective to see familiar things in a new light. This might mean looking at an object from a different angle or appreciating the way light interacts with your surroundings.

13. **Create Rituals**: Establish small rituals that bring comfort and joy, like a weekly tea time, a nightly book reading, or a morning stretch routine. These rituals can become cherished parts of your life, highlighting the beauty of routine.

Incorporating these practices into your daily life can help you uncover and celebrate the simple yet profound beauty that exists all around you. By fostering a mindset of appreciation and mindfulness, you'll find that the ordinary often holds extraordinary moments of joy.

From a philosophical perspective, enjoying simple things can be seen as a profound reflection of our ability to find meaning and fulfillment in the ordinary aspects of life. *Many philosophical traditions emphasize that true contentment arises not from the pursuit of grandiose achievements or material excess, but from the appreciation of life's everyday experiences.*

Epicurean Philosophy, for example, teaches that the pursuit of simple pleasures, such as friendship, nature, and personal reflection, leads to a more profound and lasting happiness than the pursuit of luxury or power. Epicurus said that by savoring modest pleasures and cultivating a tranquil state of mind, individuals could achieve a **state of ataraxia**, or **inner peace.** According to him, the pursuit of natural and necessary pleasures, such as good company, a pleasant meal, or a walk in nature, helps to reduce anxiety and promotes a sense of fulfillment.

Epicurean Philosophy suggests that the accumulation of wealth and power often leads to more complex desires and greater anxiety, rather than genuine happiness. By contrast, embracing simplicity and appreciating the modest joys of life can foster a deeper sense of satisfaction. This approach encourages individuals to cultivate a life of moderation, reflection, and gratitude, finding joy in the simplicity of their daily experiences and interactions.

In essence, Epicurean philosophy teaches that happiness is not found in the excesses of life, but in the thoughtful appreciation of what is simple and meaningful.

The Quiet Joys of Life

Mandakini Tomar

In the quiet bloom of morning light,
Happiness waits, both soft and slight.
Not in excess, nor wealth's embrace,
But in simple joys, in gentle grace.

In the stillness of a starry night,
Hope flickers softly, shining bright.
Not in grand dreams or distant goals,
But in quiet moments that soothe our souls.

A walk through nature, a heartfelt song,
Where we belong, where we feel strong.
For happiness lives in the heart's embrace,
In simple acts, in a kind embrace.
A meal well shared, a friend's kind face,
The beauty of an open space.
For life is rich in moments small,
And there, true peace awaits us all.

The Trap of Undervaluing Your Potential: Recognizing Your Worth and the World's Need for Your Gifts

The Potential Dismissal Trap

"The greatest waste in life is unfulfilled potential. Move past your doubts, step through the door of fear, and discover the life you were always meant to live."

You are capable of doing so much that you do not even know. *There is so much beauty on the other side of the door, move away from the door of doubts and crippling thoughts.* You have to cross this door to enter a new room of adventure. An unfulfilled potential is the biggest waste of life. You have one life to explore the hidden depths within you and set a name for yourself in this Universe. Often what holds you back is your doubt, fear to discover the other side of life, your mindset. **Nothing matters, not your age, not your environment, nothing; what matters is your willingness to go and discover your potential.**

The biggest mistake you can make in life is that you had the potential to grow, you had the gifts, you had the potential to work on your passion, you had the resources, you had the time, you had unflinching support, yet you chose to follow the laid-down path carved by others. It is the most crippling of all mistakes and the biggest trap. So, when you see other people successful, happy, and following their heart, then you do not have the right to say, "I could have also done this". You do not have the right to feel bad because you made the mistake of not understanding what you were capable of.

The society lays down a trap where they act as the carpenter. If you have heard of two different parenting styles – the carpenter parent thinks a child can be molded. The carpenter is continuously trying to give a certain shape to the raw wood. A highly controlled approach where parents shape their children's lives in a very specific way. Over-involved and overprotective, they do not allow you to take risks. Absolutely no autonomy is given, and the children become less risk-taking, forcing them to kill their dreams. Carpenter parents might impose their own dreams and expectations onto their children, leading to a lack of genuine personal fulfillment and a disconnect between what the child truly wants and what they are pursuing.

What we need is gardeners and not carpenters. Gardeners provide a good ecosystem. This approach is more about nurturing and supporting a child's growth rather than dictating it. Gardener parents provide guidance and resources, allowing children to explore their own interests and learn from their experiences. They provide good conditions, only hoping for the best. But they know that plants will grow by themselves.

Break free from the trap of being molded by others. Instead, seek guidance that empowers you to discover your own path. True growth comes not from conformity, but from the freedom to explore, learn, and evolve on your own terms.

Embracing the Journey: Be Fearless, Be Curious, Be You

Do not fall into the trap when you see carpenters around you. Look for gardeners and be a gardener. Be fearless, be curious to learn and explore yourself. *You are your biggest project. It is disappointing when people back out from their dream.* If you dare to follow your dream, follow your hunches and share your gifts with the world, then there will be a lot of people who will look up to you. You should work to listen to that applause, work for that appreciation, or whatever gives you a kick. You might as well work for your self-satisfaction, sense of accomplishment, or victory. Have the courage. Develop courage. Courage is like a muscle, use it daily to make it strong. **"Courage is not a single leap but a series of steps taken despite fear. With each step, your strength**

and confidence grow". Only courageous and fearless people can follow their dream. You have to become deaf to judgments. Judgments from others can be paralyzing. They may instill self-doubt, create a fear of failure, and make you second-guess your choices. *The fear of not meeting others' expectations can divert you from your path and diminish your motivation.* While feedback can be valuable, external judgments are often based on the perspectives and limitations of others, not on your true potential or vision. Judgments can exacerbate self-doubt, making you question your abilities and decisions. This can lead to hesitation and a reluctance to pursue your dreams.

Follow your inner voice and not the timid voices of the world. They are the same people who would want to be associated with you when you achieve something in life.

As an individual soul, you have a responsibility toward yourself wherein you need to honor your potential, inclination, skills, talent, dream, vision, education, or simply your being. Through sharing your gifts, even if you can inspire or touch the life of even one soul, you have walked the path of glory. ***Somebody who is lesser than you on all the above aspects will never want you to follow your dream.*** People's reactions to your dreams are often influenced by their own insecurities and limitations. Those who feel threatened or uncertain about their own aspirations may react negatively to your ambitions. Individuals who are insecure about their own potential may project their fears onto you. They might feel threatened by your success or fear that your achievements will highlight their own shortcomings. Their reactions are often more about their own experiences than about you personally. Remember that following your dreams is about personal fulfillment and growth. Your journey is uniquely yours, and staying connected to your own values and desires helps maintain motivation.

Isn't it weird that often people give too much weight to the opinions of other people who did not even have an idea of what you are or were capable of? You give too much power into the hands of others. **"It's quite strange how we often let the opinions of those who know little about our true potential hold so much power over our choices. Remember, their judgments reflect their limitations, not your possibilities."**

Would you care about it after 5 years, 10 years, or 15 years of what people thought of you? Think of proving them wrong. Think of showing your new side to them. Think of what it would be like when you could reach out to so many other souls through sharing your gifts. Make the world a better place by sharing your gifts.

The World's Need for Your Gifts

Your gifts are part of your soul's mission, an integral aspect of your spiritual journey. Embracing these talents means aligning with your soul's purpose and contributing to the greater good. The world benefits from the diverse talents and perspectives each individual brings. *By recognizing how your unique gifts can address needs and create positive change, you can align your efforts with broader societal impacts.* Using your gifts not only fulfills your personal destiny but also serves the divine plan. Spiritual fulfillment will only come to you from living in accordance with your true nature and purpose. Turn deaf to the noise of others' opinions and advice. True clarity comes from within. Align with your own purpose, trust your gifts, and let your actions be guided by your inner truth, not the distractions of the outside world.

Impact of Individual Contributions with their Unique Gifts

- **Filling Gaps:** Your unique skills and insights can fill gaps that others might not be able to address. Whether it's a new idea, a creative solution, or a compassionate approach, your contributions are valuable to society.

- **Inspiring Change:** By embracing your gifts and sharing them with the world, you have the potential to inspire and uplift others. Your actions can motivate others to recognize and utilize their own talents, creating a ripple effect of positive change.

- **Creating Positive Change:** The positive changes you create through your gifts resonate with the spiritual fabric of the Universe. Your contributions help manifest a higher level of consciousness and collective evolution.

Divine Gifts

In the quiet dawn, where shadows blend,

There's a truth that waits, a message to send.

A spark within, both bright and true,

A gift of light, bestowed upon you.

Do not doubt the strength you hold,

Nor shy away from dreams untold,

For in your heart, a light does gleam,

A thread of hope, a woven dream.

The Divine, in wisdom grand,

Crafted you with a guiding hand.

Each talent, skill, and every grace,

A piece of heaven's soft embrace.

When self-doubt whispers dark and deep,

Remember, the soul's worth is yours to keep.

Embrace your gifts, both great and small,

For in your purpose, you stand tall.

Your path may wind, your journey may twist,

Yet in your spirit, never miss.

The truth that you are meant to shine,

To share your light, to seek, to find.

The world awaits your soul's true song,

A melody where hearts belong.

So rise, with faith and courage strong,

And let your gifts in joy prolong.

For in each act of love and care,

The Divine's light shines everywhere.

Through you, His grace and purpose flow,

A beacon bright to guide and show.

So honor now the spark you bear,

And trust in blessings, rich and rare.

Your worth is etched in stardust, bright,

A gift divine, a guiding light.

Embrace your journey with confidence, knowing that your pursuit of dreams contributes to a broader narrative of courage and possibility. By overcoming discouragement and remaining steadfast, you pave the way for your own success and set an example for others to follow.

Enlightening Wisdom

A List of the Different Spiritual Gifts as Per Bible

- **Wisdom** - The supernatural ability to think with godly wisdom in accordance with the Scriptures.

- **Teaching** - The supernatural ability to teach the Word of God in an accurate and understandable way.

- **Shepherding** – The supernatural ability to pastor and shepherd God's Church as an under-shepherd of our chief shepherd.

- **Mercy** - The supernatural ability to show mercy and compassion to people in your life, even those who have wronged you or don't seem to deserve it.

- **Leadership** - The supernatural ability to lead God's people to follow Him and to equip others to do the work of the ministry.

- **Knowledge** - The supernatural ability to discern even difficult theological truths and to have a capacity for learning and remembering them.

- **Intercession** - The supernatural ability to pray without ceasing. To often react to situations with prayer as a first response.

- **Hospitality** - The supernatural ability to care for others and refresh their souls by serving them in some way, even to want to do this for strangers.

- **Helps** - The supernatural ability to want to serve others and ensure that all perceived needs are met. Not being able to sit back when there is work to be done.

- **Giving** - The supernatural desire to want to be generous and the dedication to actually follow through. This is not limited to, but certainly includes, financial giving.

- **Faith** - The supernatural ability to trust the Lord in all things. While others tend to worry often, you have a strong faith even in the midst of worry.

- **Evangelism** - The supernatural ability and desire to reach lost people. Of course, all believers should have this, but those with this spiritual gift stand out in this area and have an extra level of zeal.

- **Encouragement** - The supernatural ability to encourage others and build them up. When others spend time around you, they often walk away feeling encouraged.

- **Discernment** - The supernatural ability to determine right from wrong and truth from error.

- **Administration** - The supernatural ability to guide others and help organize plans for the furtherance of the ministry. This is more than those who have a natural bent toward organization; it's those who seem to be able to discern what's most important to focus on and are gifted to help implement strategies to that end.

The Trap of Being Timid in Life and not Learning from the Hints Dropped by Universe

The Trap of Timidity

"In shadows deep, our fears reside,
But the light of courage can turn the tide."

You know what makes a life happy and fulfilling; it is your ability to learn continuously from your experiences and evolve. Life is nothing but a series of lessons. The moment we stop being aware, observe, and learn is when we stop growing. There are lessons hidden at every point. *Do not wait for something big to happen. Do not wait for something to shake you up, and then you go into your shell wondering why things happened the way they did.* Once you get your lessons, memory fades, and you go back to your normal course of life. *But the actual lesson is to never forget the lessons.* You become a weak person without your learnings. If you want to evolve, you will have to come out of your comfort zone.

You have to be aware of what is happening to you and what is happening around you. You have to make amends, change, and mold after learning the happenings around you. If you fail to change, you will find yourself witnessing the same set of issues. You have to break the cycles of monotony, negative emotions, failure, or anything that disturbs the peace of your mind.

Sometimes when you get your lessons, you will realize it is a way to help you upgrade into a better version. That lesson then becomes a true blessing.

For example, if you do not speak up for yourself, if you are too timid, if you are an over-giver, then life will throw you into a situation where ultimately, to lift yourself higher up or to save yourself, you will have no choice but to speak up for yourself. Constantly, you will face situations where the only way to come out of the trap would be to stop being timid and be more audacious. Do not be afraid of confrontation and of standing up for yourself. Otherwise, do not regret later being taken advantage of and being treated poorly by others. The Universe wants you to face your fears and be more assertive and confident.

The Trap of Timidity

It's all too easy to get stuck in a cycle of timidity. Life can feel overwhelming, and when opportunities arise, fear often steps in, whispering doubts that hold us back. This can lead to missed chances for growth and connection.

Hints from the Universe

The Universe communicates with us in subtle ways, through synchronicities, feelings, and sometimes even challenges. These hints can feel like nudges, urging us to take a leap or explore a new path. *For example, you might keep running into the same topic or idea, or maybe you have a gut feeling that something is worth pursuing or something is not fine.* Ignoring these signals can lead to a sense of stagnation or regret.

When you are an over-giver, the Universe will turn your favorite person into a lesson. In the midst of all this, you will learn to rely on yourself and be your own refuge, know where to stop being nice, maintain boundaries, not trust too much, or you will be forced to learn to find your own beauty. Once you discover your beauty, you will forge new connections, move in the right direction. You will learn to take delight in the Lord.

"Take delight in the Lord, and he will give you the desires of your heart. Commit your way to the Lord; trust in him, and he will do this: He will make your righteous reward shine like the dawn, your vindication like the noonday sun." – Psalm 37:4-6

Many people stay in the trap because they fail to understand the signs of the Universe. They fail to understand the lessons or implement them from time to time. It's important to cultivate awareness and bravery, even in small steps.

Embracing vulnerability allows for growth. *Each time you step out of your comfort zone, even slightly, you learn something new about yourself and what you're capable of.* Reflecting on past experiences can also help; what did you notice when you took risks? What did you learn?

It's all about balance: listening to your intuition while pushing through fear. The more you engage with life, the more you'll discover what the Universe is trying to show you. How do you feel about taking small steps to break out of that timidity? Taking small steps to break free from timidity is incredibly powerful. It's about gradually building confidence, one action at a time. Every small step, no matter how seemingly insignificant, adds up to a shift in mindset. The key is to start with what feels manageable, push past discomfort, and celebrate progress. In time, those tiny steps become giant strides toward a more empowered and authentic version of yourself. It's not about instant transformation; it's about consistent growth.

Enlightening Wisdom

As per Hinduism, every soul is born with a purpose. The soul takes birth to complete the lessons, which it could not learn during previous births. So, every birth is a chance to learn the lessons, keep pushing the limits using intellect and spiritual strength, and move toward higher consciousness. The more lessons you learn spiritually, the better it is for your soul's expansion and growth. The more lessons you embrace and learn, the more your soul expands. Be courageous in life, dare to face challenges, grow from them, and move steadily toward spiritual enlightenment. Every step forward is a step closer to the fullness of your soul's potential.

Just as a spider weaves its own web out of itself and sits at the center of it, we create our own world by projecting our thoughts, words, and actions outside. The entire creation is bound up with name and form and is thus unreal. It can be described in words, so it is limited and circumscribed by the intellect and the mind. *True consciousness lies beyond the duality of pleasure and pain, praise and ridicule, loss or gain, desire and attachments.* Someone appears to us as a friend or a foe depending on the projection of our own egotistical mind and its multifarious likes and dislikes. We are fearful of this world just as one would who imagines a snake in place of a rope in a dimly lit room. The moment he lights a lamp and sees the rope for what it is, his fear vanishes immediately.

Just as light dispels darkness, courage illuminates our path, helping us navigate through challenging situations. "Turn the tide" act with courage, you can change our circumstances and overcome obstacles.

Do Not Be Timid
By Mandakini Tomar

In the quiet moments, when doubts creep in,
Remember the fire that burns within.
You've faced the storms, felt the weight,
But your spirit is strong, your heart innate.

Stand firm in your truth, let your voice ring,
Each word a note, let your story sing.
You've walked through shadows, emerged with light,
A testament to courage, a beautiful sight.

Embrace your journey, every twist and turn,
In the lessons learned, let your spirit burn.
You are more than the fears that bind,
A tapestry of dreams, uniquely designed.

So when the world feels heavy and vast,
Know that your presence is a spell cast.
Do not be timid; let your essence shine,
For you are a miracle, so pure and divine.

The Trap of Losing Yourself or Your Identity in Societal Pressures or Relationships (The Butterfly in a Jar)

Trap of Diluting your Identity

O ne of the biggest regrets that you can have in life when you look back is that you lost yourself in the process called life.

> **In the rush of days, don't lose your spark,**
>
> **Amidst the noise, don't let your heart grow dark.**
>
> **Life's a fleeting journey, a delicate dance,**
>
> **Hold tight to your dreams; give your soul a chance.**
>
> **For when the years fade and you look back to see,**
>
> **Regret whispers softly, "You forgot to be free."**

Often, people lose their sense of direction, perspective, focus, and deviate from their principles when confronted with the negativity of people or societal pressures.

In a world buzzing with expectations and standards, the pressure to conform can feel overwhelming. Many individuals find themselves lost, drifting away from their true selves in a sea of societal norms.

It is so hard to retain your identity, yet it is the most crucial and satisfying thing to do in life. There are people who will constantly try to drain your energy, pull you into their negativity trap, and pull you down to show you that you don't matter. *These people can make you fall into a trap by misdirecting your energy. You have to be vigilant enough to not let your energy be misdirected, and every effort should be made to retain your identity.*

Ignore the drama of people and sail through this journey called life by being yourself. Make your attention and time a very precious thing. Do not just give it away to anyone. The time that you waste in people-pleasing, deviating from your goals, will not come back. Toxic people or society are not worth your time; you go on losing yourself trying to change to fit their ideal image or conform to their standards. Someone's idea of a perfect you is not your responsibility to fulfill. Do you know the cost of conformity?

The Cost of Conformity is Huge Leading to

1. **Identity Crisis**:

    o   Changing yourself to meet someone else's expectations can lead to an identity crisis. You may start to feel like a stranger to yourself, questioning who you really are and what you truly value.

2. **Emotional Toll**:

    o   Constantly molding yourself to fit others' ideals can be exhausting. This emotional labor can lead to anxiety, stress, and a deep sense of dissatisfaction.

3. **Superficial Connections**:

    o   When you're not being authentic, the connections you form may be shallow. Genuine relationships are built on honesty and acceptance; pretending to be someone you're not prevents true intimacy.

To try to fulfill everyone's expectations and conform to their standards is a trap. Nurture and preserve yourself without getting caught in societal expectations, pressures, or demands of day-to-day life. *Your authenticity is like a badge that you should wear proudly*. Apart from your livelihood, keep yourself engaged in activities that bring you genuine joy and fulfillment. Tell me, what, according to you, is misery? You feel miserable when you lose touch with yourself. You fall into deep pits of sadness because you are not able to reconnect with your authentic self. You do not have an idea of what you want to do, what gives you happiness, where you went wrong, what brings you fulfillment. You will not have anything to fall back on when you want to reconnect with yourself.

Sometimes People Also Lose Themselves in Relationships: How?

- They stop doing things outside the relationship like spending time with friends, pursuing their hobbies, etc. In a close relationship, personal development may take a backseat. Failing to engage in self-care, hobbies, or friendships can result in a feeling of stagnation and disconnection from one's true self.

- It's common for partners to influence each other, but when one partner's interests, beliefs, or values become dominant, the other may start to adopt them at the expense of their own identity. They become too obsessed with the feelings of others and their needs rather than their own. Being considerate of others' feelings is fine, but becoming obsessed leads to losing yourself.

- They resist change or growth out of a fear of hurting others or being too far ahead, which might displease the other person.

- They start compromising on the values, beliefs, and morals to make things work.

- They aren't able to spend time alone.

- The fear of upsetting a partner, friend, family member or losing the relationship causes individuals to suppress their true feelings or opinions. This avoidance can create a façade that distances them from their authentic self.

- Many individuals define themselves by their roles within a relationship, such as being a parent, partner, or caretaker. When these roles overshadow personal interests and values, it can lead to feeling lost.

The best gift you can give to yourself is to get out of the trap of losing yourself. The best gift is to get in touch with yourself. You have to find the right balance between maintaining your individuality and nurturing connections.

What to Do?

- Make time for activities that bring you joy and fulfillment. Pursuing your interests helps reinforce your identity.

- Never stop doing what you are good at, i.e. painting, dancing, writing, cooking, designing – anything that brings you fulfillment.

- Dedicate regular time for yourself to recharge and reflect. This can be as simple as a walk, reading, or meditation.

- Do not let the opinions of others overpower you.

- Stay connected with friends and family outside of your romantic relationship. Having a support network helps you feel grounded.

- Follow your inner voice.

- Do not let the opinions of others dim your light.

- Be your own mentor and stay true to your passion, even when others do not understand it.

- The world will push you to conform to its standards, but do not give in.

- Keep reminding yourself, "My worth is not defined by others' opinions about me."

- Be happy with being you.

- Being yourself means walking alone, so do not be afraid to walk alone.

- You should know when to unplug from the chaos.

- You should listen to your intuition. What works for others might not work for you.

The Butterfly in a Jar

Imagine a butterfly trapped inside a jar. At first, it flutters around, beautiful and vibrant. But over time, it starts to adapt to the confines of the jar, altering its movements to fit the limited space. But is the butterfly truly meant to fly in a jar? Is that her true nature? Initially, it may try to spread its wings fully, but as it encounters the walls repeatedly, it learns to minimize its movements, becoming cautious and constrained.

In relationships, individuals can feel similarly confined when they suppress their true selves to avoid conflict or maintain the status quo. The fear of disapproval or rejection can lead to a gradual change in behavior, where one starts to prioritise their partner's needs and expectations over their own. Just as the butterfly may forget how to fly freely, people in relationships might lose sight of their passions, values, and dreams.

Over time, they may become so accustomed to this limited existence that they no longer remember what it feels like to be fully themselves: beautiful, vibrant, and unencumbered. They might adapt so thoroughly that their authentic selves feel like a distant memory, overshadowed by the desire to fit into the confines of the relationship. As they change to fit the constraints of the relationship, they risk losing the essence of who they are, just like the butterfly that forgets how to soar.

Overcome the Trap: The Importance of Freedom

Recognizing this dynamic is essential for maintaining one's identity within relationships. It highlights the need for self-awareness and open communication. Just as the butterfly requires the freedom to soar, individuals must seek environments—both within and outside relationships—where they can thrive without compromising their essence. While circumstances may shape us, it is our choices that define who we become. *Embracing your true self requires conscious effort, courage, and the freedom to express your individuality— just like the butterfly must break free from the jar to soar into the open sky.*

The Butterfly's Song
Mandakini Tomar

In a jar where whispers softly dwell,

A butterfly dances, caught in a shell.

Once vibrant and free, it soared through the air,

Now it flutters in silence, trapped in despair.

Its colors once bright, a radiant hue,

Fade slowly with doubt, like morning dew.

Each tap on the glass is a reminder of fear,

As it learns to be small, it forgets to be near.

But deep in its heart, a spark still remains,

A whisper of freedom, despite all the chains.

With courage, it dreams of the skies up above,

Where it can spread its wings and rediscover love.

So, let not your spirit be trapped in a jar,

For true connection blooms when you know who you are.

Embrace every color, let your essence unfold,

In the dance of authenticity, be brave and be bold.

Break free from the confines, let your true self shine,

Like a butterfly soaring, your spirit is divine.

For life's sweetest moments are found in the light,

When you honor your journey and take flight with delight.

Trap of not Being Bold Enough in Life

Not being bold is the biggest trap in life. If you are not bold enough, you will have regrets about chances that were not taken. Even if you are or were capable enough but you could not muster up the courage to follow your dreams like going abroad to study, not taking up a job that was not in your comfort area, choosing the wrong field to play it safe, making choices as per society to play it safe again. Being bold is a prerequisite for a great life.

You don't act bold because you want to be the goody-goody person, an extremely nice person. You do not want to displease or offend people in one way or another. So, you have to be bold enough in life. Only the mediocre want to be liked by everyone. **"Only the mediocre seek the approval of all; the extraordinary embrace their true selves and inspire through authenticity."** Great men and noble persons do not crave attention or liking.

Chasing approval from everyone leads to mediocrity. It keeps you from making difficult choices and prevents you from addressing the tough conversations that are necessary for growth.

When you are not bold enough, you will avoid tough decisions in life, you will avoid confronting people when needed, you will not be a man of your word, you will not show up when needed, you will only believe in playing it safe. **Being bold requires you to be different from most people. Bold people are so full of self-love and confidence that they are not afraid to be themselves.** Even if they make mistakes, they own them and build themselves from such mistakes. They have the courage to say no and to accept a no, embrace their individuality and stand by their opinions. The other side of fear is boldness and love.

The Other Side of Fear: Boldness and Love

Fear often stands as a formidable barrier in our lives, influencing our decisions and shaping our experiences. **Yet, on the other side of that fear lies a profound potential for boldness and love.** Love, whether for ourselves or for others, can propel us beyond fear. When we act from a place of love, we are more likely to take risks, pursue our passions, and advocate for our beliefs. Love ignites a sense of purpose that can overshadow fear. Engaging in acts of love—whether through compassion, kindness, or support—can help you heal from the wounds inflicted by fear. Love cultivates a sense of belonging and acceptance, reminding us that we are not alone in our struggles.

Once you come out of the safety net, the world out there waits for you. Do not be terrified. Do not be discouraged. ***For God will be with you and not people's opinion.*** *You will face rejection, people doubting you, alienating you, ignoring you, but you concentrate on your goal.*

The Game of Life: Embracing Attempts

Like the game of basketball, what matters is trying to make the shot. It doesn't matter if you missed or scored. It's not just about scoring; it's about the courage to attempt, learn, and grow—because every shot taken brings you one step closer to mastery. In basketball, what truly matters is the willingness to take the shot. Each attempt, whether it results in a score or a miss, contributes to your journey as a player. Any experienced player was once a novice.

- **The Courage in Attempting:**
  - Just like in basketball, life requires us to take risks and make attempts. Success isn't defined solely by the outcomes; it's about the courage to step up when the moment feels right. Each attempt teaches us something valuable, regardless of the result.

- **Learning from Mistakes:**
  - Every missed shot is an opportunity for learning. Experienced players analyse their mistakes, adjusting their techniques and strategies for future attempts. **Similarly, in life, setbacks offer lessons that help us grow and improve.**

- **Progress Over Perfection:**
  - No one becomes a skilled player overnight. Every experienced athlete was once a novice, understanding that mastery comes with practice and perseverance. It's essential to focus on progress rather than perfection, celebrating small victories along the way.

- **Timing and Intuition:**
  - Knowing when to take the shot is crucial. It requires a blend of intuition, practice, and awareness of the game. In life, trusting your instincts and recognizing the right moments to act can lead to rewarding experiences.

Little Acts of Boldness

You develop the skill of being bold by doing small acts of boldness in life. It can be: trying a new hobby, saying sorry, allowing yourself to be vulnerable, detesting bad behavior by someone, going out of your way to help someone, intending to be yourself, and listening to your inner conscience.

Boldness = Intention + Confidence + Action.

Three of the traits go hand in hand. If you have intention but no confidence, you will not be able to act. If you want to act but the intention is not clear, it again won't serve the purpose.

ENLIGHTENING WISDOM

In Hindu tradition, courage (shauriya) and patience (dhairya) are among the first of the ten qualities of dharma outlined in the Manusmṛti. Along with forgiveness (kshama), self-control (dama), honesty (asteya), sanctity (shauch), control of the senses (indraiya-nigrah), reason (dhi), knowledge (vidya), truthfulness (satya), and absence of anger (krodha), these virtues guide one's path toward righteousness. Embrace courage as a fundamental force to follow your true path, for it is through brave action and steadfast patience that we fulfill our dharma and elevate our lives. Courage is not just physical bravery but encompasses mental and emotional fortitude as well. It involves standing up for what is right, protecting righteousness, and embracing challenges with a fearless heart.

The **Mahabharata**, in particular, highlights courage as the strength to fight against injustice and uphold truth, even in the face of overwhelming odds.

Arjuna's courage is tested not just on the battlefield, but in overcoming his **mental and emotional blockages**. His true courage emerges when he listens to Krishna's wisdom, gains clarity about his purpose, and is able to transcend his fear and doubt. Krishna's teachings help Arjuna realize that true courage is not just the absence of fear but the ability to act in alignment with **dharma** and higher spiritual truths, even when faced with difficult or painful choices. Arjuna's willingness to overcome his emotional turmoil and follow Krishna's guidance marks his growth from a warrior who was driven by duty alone to one who acts in alignment with higher spiritual wisdom.

The Courage to Act:

- Once Arjuna gains clarity, he finds the courage to fight. He no longer sees the battle as a personal vendetta but as a divine mission to restore **dharma** and righteousness in the world.

- With new found wisdom and determination, Arjuna steps back onto the battlefield, ready to fulfill his duty as a warrior. He fights not out of anger or vengeance but from a place of **spiritual alignment** with the will of the divine.

- His courage is thus a combination of physical bravery and the spiritual strength to act in accordance with **divine will** and **cosmic order**.

Lord Hanuman

Lord Hanuman is the God of courage in Indian mythology. He has the courage of the raging wind.

Hanuman Ji is associated with courage and in moments of utter despair, people pray to Lord Hanuman to give them the strength to bear any problem bravely. Hanuman Ji's strength is one of his greatest powers. He alone can take on an entire army. He faced numerous formidable challenges without fear. His willingness to confront powerful foes like Ravana illustrates that true courage is not the absence of fear, but the ability to act in the face of it. He teaches us that facing our fears head-on is essential for personal growth.

He can cross oceans and uproot entire mountains. The magnitude of Hanuman Ji's strength is unparalleled by any other god or human in Hindu mythology. Lord Hanuman's courage also inspires others around him. His fearless nature instills confidence in the troops of Lord Rama, motivating them to fight for justice. This shows that courage can be contagious; by being brave ourselves, we can encourage and uplift those around us.

"Through Hanuman Ji's unwavering spirit, we learn that true courage is not just in grand gestures, but in the quiet strength to face challenges, serve others, and remain true to our values."

TRAP NO. 11

The Trap of Chasing the Wrong Things

Trap of Chasing Illusions

"Chasing the wrong things in life is like running on a treadmill – endless effort with no true progress; true fulfillment comes from aligning your pursuits with your deepest values."

How can the right things catch you if you do not stop chasing wrong things in life? The biggest trap of life is to waste your life on things that do not even matter and will never matter when you look back. Time wasted is the biggest regret a lot of people have. *There is a famous saying: "If you do not plan your time, somebody else will help you waste it."* Time is more precious than money. You often fall into the trap of:

1. Chasing Wrong People

If you invest your time and energy in chasing the wrong people, you may find yourself caught in a cycle of unfulfilled expectations. *These individuals can consume your thoughts and overshadow what truly matters, leaving you little room to focus on your own goals and aspirations.* Over time, you might realize that these connections aren't genuine, and that you never received the attention or support you sought. Ultimately, this can feel like a trap—one that distracts you from the relationships and opportunities that truly deserve your energy. It's essential to recognize when your efforts are misplaced and to redirect your focus toward those who genuinely appreciate you.

2. Chasing Wrong Goals

You waste a part of your life in chasing wrong or unrealistic goals only to regret later that it was the biggest trap to fall in. When you chase wrong goals and you still achieve them it keeps you joyless and a pang of unfulfillment still resides in your heart. *Chasing unrealistic or misguided goals can lead you to waste precious years of your life, only to look back with regret and realize it was a significant trap.* As the saying goes, "Not all that glitters is gold." Even if you achieve these goals, the victory often feels hollow, leaving a lingering sense of unfulfillment. For example, consider someone who dedicates years to climbing the corporate ladder, believing that a high-paying job will bring happiness. Once they reach that position, they might find themselves feeling joyless, as the stress and lack of passion overshadow any financial gain. The fulfillment they sought remains elusive, and they realize too late that they sacrificed their true interests and passions in the process. Another common scenario is pursuing societal standards of success, like having a certain lifestyle or status. Many chase these superficial markers only to discover they don't align with their true values or desires. As philosopher Alan Watts said, "The more a thing tends to be permanent, the more it tends to be lifeless." When you pursue goals that don't resonate with your authentic self, you risk becoming trapped in a cycle of dissatisfaction. Ultimately, it's crucial to reflect on your aspirations and ensure they align with your true self. Investing in goals that resonate with your passions and values can lead to a more fulfilling and meaningful life. *By focusing on what truly matters to you, you can avoid the regret that often accompanies chasing the wrong goals.*

3. Chasing Outer Beauty and Ignoring Inner Beauty

In a world that often emphasizes physical appearance, it's easy to overlook the profound significance of inner beauty. While outer beauty is fleeting, spiritual beauty—the beauty of the mind and soul—has the power to resonate deeply with others. As the saying goes, "Beauty is only skin deep," and true beauty radiates from qualities like love, joy, grace, gentleness, and a positive attitude.

Have you ever encountered someone whose spirit felt beautiful? Perhaps it was their genuine smile, the glint in their eyes, or their empathetic nature. These qualities transcend mere physical characteristics; they reflect a well-nurtured inner self. As the Buddha said, "The mind is everything. What you think, you become." Cultivating inner beauty involves working on your energetic system and chakras, alongside caring for your physical appearance. After all, **"A good package without good content is not worth it."**

Instead of obsessing over outer beauty, we should focus on nurturing our minds and souls. Engaging in self-care activities—like yoga, meditation, creative pursuits, and mindful eating—can help you radiate confidence and inner peace. The Bible reminds us, "Charm is deceptive, and beauty is fleeting; but a woman who fears the Lord is to be praised" (Proverbs 31:30). This emphasizes the importance of cultivating a character that reflects your values.

Self-awareness is key to develop inner beauty. Explore your interests and develop a strong character, especially in times of adversity, as character forms the foundation of your inner beauty. This beauty blossoms over time, enriched by life experiences and challenges.

To stay on the right path in life, appreciate and treasure the inner beauty in others, while cultivating it within yourself. As you do, you will leave a spark of your beautiful light wherever you go, echoing the words of Rumi: **"The wound is the place where the Light enters you."** Embrace both your inner and outer beauty, and strive for a balance that enriches your life and the lives of those around you. To be on the right track in life, appreciate the inner beauty in people, treasure such people, and cultivate it within yourself. If you do so, you will leave a spark of your beautiful light wherever you go.

THE LIGHTHOUSE

Think of a lighthouse standing tall on a rocky shore. Its bright light symbolizes inner beauty—the guiding force that helps others navigate through life's storms. The exterior of the lighthouse, with its paint and structure, represents outer beauty. While it's important for the lighthouse to look appealing and be visible, its true purpose lies in the light it emits.

The lighthouse can be beautifully designed, but if it doesn't shine brightly, it won't fulfill its mission. Similarly, we can invest time and effort in our outer appearance, but without cultivating the light of our inner qualities—like kindness, compassion, and integrity—we lack the true essence that guides and inspires others.

When a storm hits, what matters most isn't how pretty the lighthouse looks, but how brightly it shines to lead ships safely home. In our own lives, focusing solely on outer beauty can leave us unprepared for life's challenges. However, when we nurture our inner beauty, we become beacons of hope and strength for ourselves and those around us.

By embracing this balance, we can become lighthouses in our communities, radiating the light of our true selves while still appreciating the beauty of our outer appearance. This way, we not only shine for ourselves, but also illuminate the paths of others, creating a ripple effect of positivity and inspiration.

4. Chasing approval by people pleasing

"In the race of life, run toward your purpose, not the expectations of others; fulfillment comes from within."

Chasing approval holds you back from being true to yourself. *When you chase approval, you are always worried about people being upset with you, people not being happy about your ways of doing things.* When you seek validation, your focus shifts to what others think, leading to anxiety and a constant worry about disappointing them. This need to please—often rooted in a personality trait known as "**sociotropy**"—can leave you feeling like you're walking on a tightrope, always trying to balance others' happiness with your own.

Remember: ***"You can't win the race if you're always running after others."*** Seeking universal approval is a losing game. When you prioritize pleasing others over your own well-being, you risk draining your emotional reserves, and that's a recipe for burnout.

You are always on your toes, overly apprehensive, jittery, and all things anxious. Your primary focus shifts from You to Them. But in life, you cannot keep everyone happy. John Lydgate's words, *"you can't please all the people all of the time"* are spot on. You can't expect yourself to make everyone happy around you at the expense of your own sanity. So, *it's a bad idea to devote a major chunk of your time to seeking approval from others by depleting your emotional bank reserves.* You should create boundaries, and that will increase your willpower. Being nice or giving in any relationship is good, but when you start doing things to please and chase approval, it creates an imbalance. A strong, healthy relationship involves a certain degree of reciprocity. Healthy relationships require reciprocity—both parties must nurture each other. As the saying goes, **"In true friendship, both hearts are open." Such a profound piece of wisdom.** Genuine connections thrive on mutual support and understanding.

Setting boundaries becomes extremely crucial. They safeguard your emotional health and allow you to flourish without feeling depleted. As Maya Angelou wisely said, "You alone are enough. You have nothing to prove to anybody." Prioritizing your needs isn't selfish; it's essential for living a fulfilling life.

Being kind and generous is beautiful, but when it turns into people-pleasing, it creates imbalance. *Imagine a seesaw: it only works when both sides share the weight.* Relationships thrive on a balance of give and take.

Take a moment to reflect:

- Are your needs being met?
- Are you receiving the same energy you're giving?

By nurturing both yourself and those around you, you can cultivate connections that uplift and inspire. Embrace your worth and let go of the need for constant approval. When you stand firm in your truth, you'll attract those who appreciate you for who you truly are. Shine your light unapologetically, and watch how it draws the right people to you.

5. Chasing Perfection

The pursuit of perfection is another common trap. Society bombards us with images of flawless lives, whether through social media, advertising, or celebrity culture. This constant comparison can lead to feelings of inadequacy and anxiety. The idea of perfection is not only unattainable but also subjective. *What one person views as perfect may differ vastly from another's perspective.* Instead of striving for an ideal that doesn't exist, embrace your uniqueness and focus on growth and progress, knowing that flaws are part of being human.

6. Chasing Status and Recognition

The desire for social status and recognition can be intoxicating. People often chase promotions, titles, and accolades, believing that these will bring them respect and fulfillment. However, this pursuit can lead to a hollow existence, where your self-worth is tied to external validation. *True respect comes from your character and how you treat others, not from a title or position.* You would notice two personalities, sometimes one who is overly nice when outside and changes three sixty degrees when at home. With age, people can become expert at this. You might meet someone who is overly nice and charming in public, putting on a polished façade to impress others. They may go out of their way to be agreeable, offering compliments and helping hands, creating an image of the perfection. However, once they return home, a 180-degree shift can occur. The same person who exuded warmth and kindness outside with others may reveal a more irritable, critical, or even resentful side behind closed doors to a member.

Chasing the wrong things can leave you feeling unfulfilled and lost. It's important to pause and reflect on what you're pursuing. By shifting your priorities and embracing authenticity, you can create a life that is truly fulfilling and aligned with your deepest values. Chasing the right things in life is about aligning your actions with your values and aspirations. By focusing on self-acceptance, meaningful relationships, personal growth, passion, health, mindfulness, and giving back, you can create a life that is rich in purpose and joy. Remember, the journey is just as important as the destination, so savor every moment along the way.

The Trap of Seeking Validation through Relationships and Love

The Connection Seekers' Trap

In the quest for love, many become so focused on finding a partner that they lose sight of their own identity. This can result in unhealthy relationships or staying in situations that do not serve them. **Love should not be about chasing someone else's affection, but about fostering connections that enrich your life.**

In the intricate dance of life, the quest for love can often overshadow our journey toward self-discovery. *Many people become so focused on finding a partner that they lose sight of their own identity.* This fixation can lead to unhealthy relationships, where individuals find themselves in situations that no longer serve their well-being or find the wrong person. Love should never be about chasing someone else's affection; rather, it should be about nurturing connections that enrich and elevate your life.

The Foundation of Self-Love

Self-love is the bedrock upon which healthy relationships are built. It's about recognizing your intrinsic worth and cultivating a strong sense of self. Often, our struggles in love reveal our deepest wounds, guiding us back to the importance of loving ourselves first. When you prioritize your well-being, you lay the groundwork for relationships that are genuine and fulfilling.

The Importance of Personal Growth

Embracing personal growth means engaging in activities that fuel your passions and interests. This journey of self-discovery allows you to flourish as an individual, making you more attractive to others. *"In the chase for love, trust the process; every misstep brings you closer to the heart that resonates with your own."* In the quest for love, be fearless; it's in the heartbreaks that you uncover the wisdom to recognize genuine connections. Embracing this courage helps you to grow, learn, and ultimately, draw the right people into your life.

Cultivating Meaningful Connections

Instead of obsessively chasing love, focus on cultivating connections that are meaningful and reciprocal. *Healthy relationships thrive on mutual respect and understanding.* The spirit of genuine connection fosters bonds that are deep and lasting.

When you shift your mindset from chasing to attracting, you open yourself up to opportunities for authentic connections. Trust that love will often find you when you least expect it—typically in moments when you are fully engaged in your own life and passions. It's during these times of self-discovery that you become magnetic to others.

Real-Life Reflections

Imagine a soul entwined in the grasp of a relationship,
Years slip by, yet joy feels like a distant clasp.
Red flags unfurl like warnings in the breeze,
But the fear of loneliness silences the pleas.

In the name of love, they compromise their core,
Each concession dims the light they once bore.
Slowly, they fade into a shadow of their past,
Yearning for freedom, but clinging to the mask.

As days turn to months, fulfillment slips away,
What once felt like love now feels like decay.

In the silence of night, they search for their spark,
Longing to rediscover the light in the dark.

True companionship blooms in honesty and trust,
Not in sacrifice that turns love into dust.
So, let the heart speak and seek what is true,
For only then can one truly start anew.

Do not Ignore The Warning Signs

Red flags can manifest in various forms, often disguised as small issues that grow over time. These may include:

1. **Lack of Respect**: If your partner dismisses your feelings or belittles your opinions, it's a clear sign of disrespect. As the saying goes, "Respect is earned, not given." In a healthy relationship, both partners honor each other's perspectives.

2. **Communication Issues**: Effective communication is the backbone of any relationship. If you find that conversations often lead to misunderstandings or hurt feelings, it may indicate deeper problems. As the proverb reminds us, "Words are free; it's how you use them that may cost you."

3. **Emotional Unavailability**: When one partner is consistently closed off or unwilling to share their emotions, it creates a barrier. Love flourishes in an environment of vulnerability. Remember, "A closed heart is a locked door."

4. **Jealousy and Control**: A little jealousy can be normal, but excessive jealousy is a warning sign. If your partner, friend or a family member attempts to control who you spend time with or how you dress, where you go, whom you meet it can signal possessiveness. "Trust is the foundation of love," and without it, relationships crumble.

5. **Ignoring Boundaries**: If your partner constantly crosses your boundaries, it indicates a lack of respect for your autonomy. "Good fences make good

neighbors" is a saying that holds true in relationships too; boundaries help maintain respect and understanding.

When you ignore these red flags, you often find yourself in a cycle of compromise. You may convince yourself that love means sacrificing personal happiness or identity. **Over time, this can lead to a profound sense of discontent. "When the roots are deep, there is no reason to fear the wind."** Yet, when you ignore the signs, you risk uprooting ourselves entirely. It's crucial to recognize that staying in a relationship out of fear of loneliness can have dire consequences. Instead, it's important to prioritize your own well-being. Engage in self-reflection and ask yourself:

- Are you truly happy?
- Are you being your authentic self?

Remember, someone who prioritizes self-love and personal growth might focus on their passions—be it art, travel, or career aspirations. As they engage in activities that light them up, they naturally attract healthier relationships into their lives.

Embracing the Journey

In the end, the pursuit of love should never come at the cost of losing yourself. Embrace the journey of self-discovery and prioritize your own growth. The poet Maya Angelou beautifully articulated, "I've learned that people will forget what you said, people will forget what you did, but people will never forget how you made them feel." When you nurture your relationship with yourself, you create a foundation for authentic connections that enhance your life. Love should never come at the expense of your self-worth. As you embark on the journey of love, remember: *"The right person will appreciate you for who you are, not for who you pretend to be."* Embrace your true self, and let that authenticity guide you toward the connections that genuinely enrich your life.

As you embark on this journey, remember:

"Love is not a chase, but a dance;

When you find yourself, you'll take the chance.

In self-discovery, let your spirit soar,

True love will find you, and you'll want for no more."

By embracing your true self and prioritizing your happiness, you create space for love that is not just a pursuit but a beautiful complement to the wonderful life you've built for yourself. Let go of the chase and allow love to flow naturally into your life, enriching your journey and celebrating your authenticity.

Remember that self-love is the foundation of any healthy relationship. Prioritize your own well-being and personal growth, and let love flow naturally when the time is right.

Consider an individual who invests years in a relationship, staying out of fear of being alone. They overlook the consistent patterns of disrespect, emotional unavailability, and lack of communication. As time passes, they feel increasingly drained and disconnected, sacrificing their dreams and interests to maintain the status quo. They may often find themselves questioning their worth, thinking, "If I just try harder, maybe things will change."

In contrast, think of someone who chooses to prioritize self-love and personal development. They spend time exploring their passions, nurturing friendships, and engaging in activities that bring them joy. Rather than chasing love, they cultivate a strong sense of self. When the time is right, they find themselves unexpectedly meeting a partner who shares their values and interests. This connection blossoms naturally, built on a foundation of mutual respect and understanding.

While the first individual may eventually feel a sense of emptiness, the second person radiates confidence and joy, attracting relationships that enhance their life. **As they say, "When you fill your own cup, it overflows; and when you shine your light, you draw in the right souls."** The difference lies not in the pursuit of love itself, but in the journey of self-discovery that prepares one to embrace it fully.

In the end, the pursuit of love should never come at the cost of losing yourself. Embrace the journey of self-discovery and prioritize your own growth. Remember that when you nurture your relationship with yourself, you create space for authentic connections that enhance your life. Love will come, not as a chase, but as a beautiful complement to the wonderful life you've built for yourself.

Wisdom Notes
The Light in the Darkness

Many spiritual traditions speak of light as a symbol of truth and authenticity. When you prioritize self-love, you will illuminate your inner light, guiding you toward healthier relationships. However, if you remain in the shadows of unhealthy partnerships, you risk dimming that light. As Nelson Mandela said, "What counts in life is not the mere fact that we have lived. It is what difference we have made to the lives of others." By nurturing your light, you can uplift not only yourself but also those around you.

Heart As a Compass

The heart serves as a powerful compass, guiding us on our journey through life and relationships. By prioritizing self-love and listening to our heart's whispers, we navigate our paths with intention and clarity. Embrace the lessons that come from both joy and discomfort, and trust that each step brings you closer to relationships that truly resonate with your authentic self. As you honor your heart's wisdom, you'll find yourself drawn to connections that uplift and enrich your life, creating a tapestry of love and fulfillment.

Hinduism: The Heart as the Seat of the Soul

In Hinduism, the heart (or "hridaya") is considered the seat of the soul and divine consciousness. The Bhagavad Gita teaches that love and devotion (bhakti) are essential for spiritual growth. When we engage in self-love, we align ourselves with our true nature, which is love itself. In Hindu philosophy, the divine masculine and feminine energies, represented by Shiva and Shakti, illustrate the balance required in relationships. True love is seen as a harmonious union of these energies, where both partners support each other's growth.

"Where there is Shakti, there is Shiva." This phrase signifies that in a relationship grounded in self-love and mutual respect, both individuals can flourish, creating a space for divine love to manifest.

Lord Krishna, in the Gita, emphasizes the importance of self-awareness and inner peace: **"He who has no attachments can really love others, for his love is pure and divine."**

In Christianity, the heart is frequently referred to as the center of one's emotions and spiritual life. Proverbs 4:23 advises, **"Above all else, guard your heart, for everything you do flows from it."** This emphasizes the importance of protecting our hearts from influences that can lead us astray

"When love is rooted in self-awareness and mutual respect, it becomes a divine force—nurtured by the harmonious union of energies. True love flows from a heart that is pure and free from attachment, as it is in guarding the heart that we protect the essence of our spirit."

The Trap of Trusting People Easily

Trap of Misplaced Trust

Do not fall into the trap of opening your heart before allowing people to show their true colors. Judge them on all grounds as I have listed in the 'Who' section. A guy named Phaedrus said to the Greek philosopher Socrates, "Things are not always what they seem; the first appearance deceives many: the intelligence of a few perceives what has been carefully hidden." This serves as a reminder that superficial impressions can be misleading.

Sometimes people can fake smiles, nice behavior, love towards you only because of their ulterior motives. You never know the person, their experiences, their value system, and what shaped them. Sometimes people can be heartless yet pretend to be sweet. They can be selfish yet pretend to be the giver. People can be selfish and pretend to be your well-wisher. People are not always what they seem. Masks people wear create an illusion. They may offer advice, support, or kindness, but beneath it all, their actions are motivated by personal gain or ulterior motives. While their words may seem caring, their actions reveal a different story—one driven by self-interest rather than genuine concern for your well-being. It's important to recognize the difference between true compassion and those who seek to manipulate your trust for their own benefit.

The Façade of Kindness

Many individuals don masks of kindness and generosity, presenting themselves as caring and supportive. Yet, beneath this exterior, they may be driven by self-interest, seeking validation, control, or personal gain. This creates a dissonance between their words and actions, leading to confusion and disappointment for those who trust them.

The Illusion of Kindness

Consider the scenario of someone who appears supportive during our most challenging moments. They lend a listening ear, offer a shoulder to cry on, and provide assistance that feels genuine. However, as time unfolds, it may become apparent that their motives are less than altruistic. Perhaps they expect something in return—loyalty, admiration, or favors—undermining the sincerity of their initial gestures. An individual may appear loyal and trustworthy, but their actions might reveal a different story over time. This misalignment can lead to feelings of betrayal, as the illusion they created begins to unravel.

As the saying goes, **"Not all that glitters is gold."** This timeless proverb serves as a reminder that external appearances can often mask deeper truths, prompting us to look beyond the surface.

This behavior resonates deeply with the proverb **"A wolf in sheep's clothing."** It serves as a potent reminder that beneath an inviting exterior, some individuals may possess intentions that are far from benevolent. Such disguises can make it essential for us to approach new relationships with discernment and caution.

When you spend more time with people, know their daily activities, their conduct, their ethics, it is then you realize there is more than meets the eye. **Words can be deceiving, but actions reveal authenticity.** Pay attention to how someone behaves, especially in challenging situations. *Their true character often shines through when they face adversity or when they believe no one is watching.* Time is a crucial element in building understanding. The more time you spend with someone, the more you can observe their true nature. This exposure allows you to witness how they interact with others, handle challenges, and respond to various situations.

For instance, consider a colleague who seems friendly in the office but becomes dismissive when dealing with clients. Such behavior can reveal underlying traits—perhaps a lack of respect or integrity—that wouldn't be apparent in casual encounters.

Daily Conduct as a Mirror

People's daily behaviors often serve as a mirror reflecting their values and beliefs. Those who consistently demonstrate kindness, empathy, and respect, even in mundane situations, are likely to embody those qualities in more significant moments as well.

Example 1: The Social Chameleon

Imagine Sanya, who is charming and sociable at parties, always the life of the gathering. Initially, you might assume she's genuine and kind. However, as you spend more time with her, perhaps through regular coffee meet-ups or collaborative projects, you begin to notice discrepancies in her behavior.

While she radiates positivity in social settings, you observe that she often speaks negatively about others when they're not around. This duality may indicate a lack of authenticity and trustworthiness, revealing that her outward charm may mask a more complicated reality.

Daily Conduct: A Reflection of Character

People's actions in their everyday lives are often the best indicators of their true selves. By watching how someone behaves in various situations—especially mundane ones—we can gain insight into their values and ethics.

Example 2: The Quiet Helper

Consider a coworker named Dev. He seems unassuming and often keeps to himself during meetings. At first glance, one might think he's disengaged or uninterested. However, as you share projects and deadlines, you notice how he consistently takes time to help others, staying late to assist a colleague who's struggling with their workload.

His willingness to lend a hand, even when it goes unnoticed, speaks volumes about his character. This quiet commitment to supporting others reveals a depth of kindness and integrity that transcends his initial introverted demeanor. It teaches a lesson that it's not always the loudest voices that make the biggest impact.

Example 3: The Resilient Artist

Consider Ambika, an artist whose vibrant work captivates many. Initially, her colorful paintings suggest a carefree spirit. However, as you spend time exploring her studio and discussing her creative process, you learn about her struggles with mental health and the therapeutic nature of her art.

This revelation deepens your appreciation for her work; each piece tells a story of resilience and healing. By understanding the context of her artistry, you gain a profound respect for her journey and the strength it takes to express herself.

Embracing Authenticity

When we look beyond appearances, we create space for authenticity in our relationships. This deeper understanding fosters connections built on trust and respect.

Beyond the Trap

Look for consistency between what people say and what they do. **Genuine individuals will align their actions with their words, fostering trust over time.** Trust is a precious commodity, not to be given away lightly. *In a world where appearances can be deceiving, placing your faith in someone too easily can lead to disappointment and heartache. It's important to take the time to observe actions, to listen to words, and to understand intentions.* True trust is built on consistency and genuine connection, not just first impressions. By exercising caution and patience, you protect your heart and foster relationships that are rooted in sincerity and respect. Remember, it's not about being distrustful, but about valuing the trust you do extend.

In a world where appearances often dominate, taking the time to truly understand others can lead to profound revelations. By observing daily conduct, ethical choices, and the richness of personality, you can uncover the depths beyond the surface. These insights not only enrich our relationships but also foster an environment of trust and authenticity.

Recognizing Deception: Wisdom

1. **Socrates**: "Be slow to fall into friendship; but when thou art in, continue firm and constant."

   This encourages careful consideration in relationships, reminding us to take our time in understanding others before fully investing.

2. **Buddha**: "Three things cannot be long hidden: the sun, the moon, and the truth." This wisdom emphasizes that, no matter how cleverly someone tries to disguise themselves, their true nature will eventually be revealed.

3. **Confucius**: "The man who moves a mountain begins by carrying away small stones." Recognizing deceit often starts with observing small behaviors and inconsistencies over time, which can lead to a larger understanding.

4. **Khalil Gibran**: "The most beautiful things in the world cannot be seen or even touched, they must be felt with the heart."

This suggests that genuine connections and feelings reveal the truth beyond the masks people wear. Be a wise judge and do not place your trust in people easily.

"A cautious heart builds trust carefully, aware that it's a treasure worth protecting."

The Trap of Over-Commitment Trap of Overextension

The Illusion of Productivity: A Modern Trap

In a world that constantly demands our attention and energy, the pressure to say "Yes" can be overwhelming. Many of us find ourselves ensnared in a web of commitments that stretch our time, energy, and emotional bandwidth to their limits. Sometimes feeling guilty for saying no or obligated to help others can prompt you to agree to commitments even when it strains you. You can overcommit when you want to prove yourself. As an overcommitter, you will often struggle to decline new opportunities or requests, fearing disappointment or missing out on potential benefits. *But you must take on as much as the capacity you have, whether it's work, relationships, or your social life.* Going overboard will not serve the purpose. There has to be a balance. If you tend to go overboard, there are high chances that you will be undervalued or not appreciated.

The Allure of Yes in Overcommitment

The allure of saying "yes" is a powerful force, often rooted in our desire for connection, validation, and a sense of purpose. It can feel satisfying to agree to new opportunities and requests, but this impulse can quickly lead to overcommitment and overwhelm. Understanding this dynamic is crucial for maintaining balance in our lives. Understanding the psychological drivers behind the allure of saying "yes" can illuminate why many of us struggle with overcommitment. These drivers—fear of missing out (FOMO), desire for approval, and societal pressures—play a significant role in shaping our choices.

The Psychological Drivers

1. **Fear of Missing Out (FOMO)**: Fear of Missing Out is a powerful motivator that can lead us to stretch ourselves too thin. We often worry that by saying no, we might miss opportunities for personal or professional growth. The thought of being left out or seen as unhelpful can drive us to overextend ourselves. The anxiety that accompanies the idea of missing an opportunity—whether it's a career advancement, a social event, or a chance to learn something new—can make saying no feel like a risk we're not willing to take. This mindset can lead to overcommitment, leaving us overwhelmed and drained. Instead of maximizing our growth, we become scattered, diminishing the quality of our experiences and relationships.

2. **Desire for Approval**: The desire for approval is another key driver of overcommitment. Many people tie their self-worth to how others perceive them. By saying yes to every request, they seek validation and acceptance, believing that their value is contingent on their willingness to help. Over time, this can erode our mental health and lead to burnout, as we neglect our own needs in favor of others' expectations.

   Example: Consider Sam, who always volunteers for additional tasks at work. He feels that if he doesn't agree to take on extra projects, his colleagues might see him as unhelpful or lazy. This need for validation leads him to say yes, even when he's already overwhelmed.

3. **Societal Pressures:** In a culture that glorifies busyness, agreeing to take on more can feel like a badge of honor. We may equate being busy with being important, reinforcing our inclination to say yes. But true honor lies not in the constant hustle, but in finding balance—where your time, energy, and peace are respected, and your priorities align with your values.

The Social Media Façade

Social media amplifies societal pressures, showcasing curated lives that appear flawless. Take, for example, an individual who scrolls through feeds filled with friends' adventures, accomplishments, and busy lives. He feels compelled to respond to every invitation and keep up appearances, often agreeing to events he doesn't really want to attend.

It's akin to being part of a never-ending performance, where everyone feels the need to showcase their best selves. The fear of being perceived as less busy or interesting leads people to overcommit, which causes stress and burnout.

The Volunteer Enthusiast

Leena is known in her community as someone who always steps up to help. Whether it's organizing events, participating in local charities, or leading community groups, she never says no. The more she takes on, the more her friends and neighbors praise her dedication.

Think of Leena as a juggler in a circus, trying to keep multiple balls in the air. Each new commitment adds another ball to the mix. While she starts off impressively, eventually, the weight of her commitments makes it impossible to maintain her act, leading to potential burnout.

The Consequences of Societal Pressures

1. **Chronic Overwhelm**: The constant push to do more & more can lead to feelings of being perpetually overwhelmedRather than savoring our achievements, we often find ourselves trapped in a cycle of meeting constant demands, losing sight of the satisfaction that should come with our efforts.

2. **Loss of Authenticity**: As we strive to meet societal expectations, we may lose sight of our true desires and values. Our decisions become more about what others think than what we genuinely want.

3. **Deterioration of Relationships**: The more we overcommit, the less time we have for meaningful connections. Friends and family may feel neglected as we chase external validation, leading to isolation and disconnection.

Do not

- **Sacrificing Personal Needs**: If every time you are the only one who consistently puts the relationship's needs ahead of your own well-being, then you need to stop.

- **Overextending Financially**: If you take on excessive financial burdens or commitments without realistic planning, it can strain you. Do not overcommit financially.

- **Agreeing to Too Many Social Obligations**: If you are overcommitting socially, it can lead to minimizing quality time together for a couple. Sometimes you need to put a close relationship first to avoid any conflict or overwhelming feeling.

The Weight of Guilt

The weight of guilt is one of the most insidious aspects of overcommitment, rooted deeply in our desire to please others and our fear of disappointing them. One of the most insidious aspects of overcommitment is the guilt that accompanies our decisions. Saying "No" can feel like letting someone down, betraying their trust, or disappointing those who rely on us. This guilt is magnified in a culture that values busyness and productivity.

We often equate our worth with our ability to fulfill every request thrown our way. This guilt becomes a self-perpetuating cycle. The more we overcommit, the more exhausted we become, leading to a decline in the quality of our work and relationships. In turn, we feel guilty about not meeting expectations, which prompts us to take on even more commitments to compensate.

The Overflowing Cup

- **Analogy**: Imagine a cup filled to the brim with water. Every time we say yes to a new commitment without recognizing our limits, we pour more water into the cup. Eventually, it overflows, creating a mess.

- **Life Lesson**: Just like the cup, we have limits. If we don't pause to recognize when we're full, we risk overwhelming ourselves and those around us.

The House of Cards

- **Analogy**: Think of a house of cards carefully balanced. Each new commitment is another card added to the structure. If too many cards are added without stability, the whole thing risks collapsing.

- **Life Lesson**: Our lives are like this delicate structure. Too many commitments can create instability. Building a solid foundation by saying no to excess helps maintain a strong and resilient life.

The Costs of Overcommitment

The impact of overcommitment extends beyond the immediate feeling of being overwhelmed. It can affect our mental health, relationships, and overall quality of life. Chronic overcommitment often leads to:

1. **Burnout**: Continuous strain can lead to physical and emotional exhaustion. Burnout manifests in irritability, decreased motivation, and a sense of helplessness. The impact of overcommitment reaches far beyond a mere sense of being overwhelmed; it can significantly alter our mental health, relationships, and overall quality of life. Chronic overcommitment is a profound challenge that manifests in several detrimental ways.

   Burnout arises from prolonged stress and the relentless pressure of juggling too many responsibilities. The renowned psychologist Brené Brown states, ***"Daring to set boundaries is about having the courage to love ourselves even when we risk disappointing others."*** However, when our reasons for saying yes are rooted in obligation rather than genuine desire, the burden becomes unbearable.

   Imagine a candle burning at both ends. The light it produces is beautiful, but the wick quickly diminishes. Similarly, our energy can be dazzling in the short term, but without rest and balance, we risk extinguishing ourselves. Burnout manifests not only in physical fatigue but also as emotional exhaustion, irritability, and a pervasive sense of helplessness.

2. **Resentment**: When we constantly prioritize others' needs over our own, it breeds resentment. We may start feeling that our time and efforts are unappreciated, leading to conflicts with those we're trying to help. When we consistently prioritize the needs of others over our own, resentment can quietly build, like a pot on the stove that's slowly boiling over.

3. **Lost Opportunities**: Overcommitment can cloud our judgment, preventing us from recognizing or pursuing opportunities that genuinely align with our goals and values. We become so entangled in commitments that we lose sight of what truly matters. ***When we are overwhelmed, inspiration is lost, leaving us in a state of desperation.***

   Think of a ship navigating through fog. The captain becomes so focused on managing the immediate tasks that they fail to see the lighthouse guiding them to safety. Overcommitment can lead us to drift aimlessly, missing chances to align with our true path and purpose.

4. **Strained Relationships**: Friends and family may start to feel neglected as our availability dwindles. We can become distant, leading to misunderstandings and a sense of isolation. As commitments pile up, we may become emotionally withdrawn, unintentionally pushing loved ones away. This withdrawal can lead to feelings of isolation, even in the presence of those we care about. The secret to lasting happiness isn't just effective communication—it's about fostering a deep emotional connection, where understanding and empathy create the foundation for meaningful relationships.Envision a bridge that connects two islands. When we overcommit, it's like removing planks from that bridge. Initially, the connection seems stable, but over time, the gaps widen, making it difficult to cross. Strained relationships suffer from lack of attention, resulting in feelings of isolation for both sides.

Breaking the Cycle of Overcommitment

1. Self-Awareness: Recognizing Your Limits

Understanding your own capacity is the first step in breaking the cycle of overcommitment. Take time to reflect on your current commitments and assess how they align with your values and well-being.

Action Step: Keep a journal for a week, noting how you feel after each commitment. Are you energized or drained? This awareness can help you identify patterns and recognize when to say No.

2. Prioritization: Focus on What Matters

Not all commitments are created equal. Learning to prioritize your tasks can help you focus on what truly matters and let go of less important obligations.

Action Step: Create a list of your current commitments and categorize them by importance and urgency. Use the Eisenhower Matrix to help distinguish between what's urgent and what's truly important.

The Eisenhower Matrix is a way to organize tasks by urgency and importance, so you can effectively prioritize your most important work.

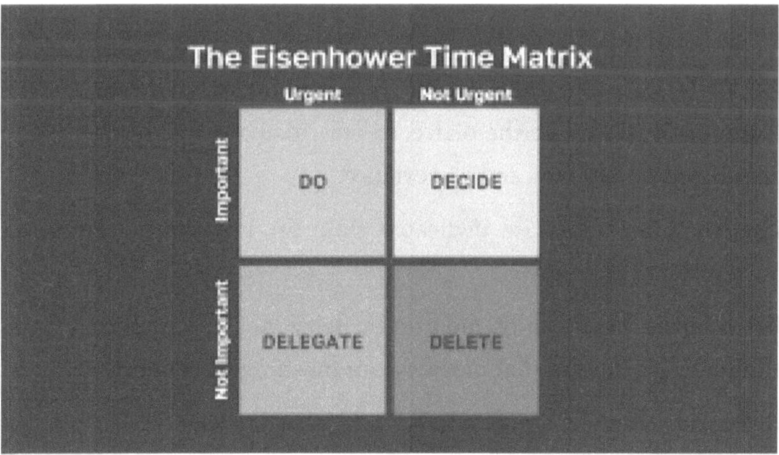

The Eisenhower Matrix is a way to organize tasks by urgency and importance, so you can effectively prioritize your most important work.

	Urgent	Not Urgent
Important	**DO** If a task is urgent and important, prioritize it. This is your highest priority task.	**SCHEDULE** If a task is important but not urgent, schedule a time to get it done.
Not Important	**DELEGATE** If a task does not require your input but does need to be done, delegate it.	**DELETE** If a task is neither urgent nor important, it should be deleted and removed from your plate.

Create an Action Plan: Based on your matrix, create a plan of action:

- Focus on completing tasks in Quadrant I.

- Schedule time for Quadrant II tasks to ensure that they receive attention.

- Delegate or minimize involvement in Quadrant III tasks.

- Eliminate or defer Quadrant IV tasks to free up time for what truly matters.

Application:

- **Communication**: Use the matrix to prioritize communication with loved ones based on urgency and importance.

- **Quality Time**: Allocate dedicated time for important relationships to nurture them and prevent neglect.

- **Boundaries**: Establish boundaries by delegating less important tasks and eliminating activities that detract from meaningful connections.

- **Reflection**: Regularly review how you're investing your time in relationships to ensure alignment with your values and goals.

By applying the Eisenhower Matrix to personal relationships, you can enhance communication, strengthen bonds and create a healthier balance between urgent demands and important priorities in your personal life.

3. Set Clear Boundaries

Establishing boundaries is essential to maintaining a healthy balance between your commitments and personal life. Clearly communicating your limits to others can help manage their expectations.

- **Action Step**: Practice saying "No" in low-stakes situations to build your confidence. Start with small requests and gradually work up to more significant ones, articulating your reasons with kindness.

Example: Saying No to a Social Event

- **Situation**: A family member invites you to a gathering, but you've been needing some alone time.
- **Response**: "Thanks for inviting me! I'm going to take this weekend to recharge, but I'd love to join next time."
- **Why it works**: You express gratitude and politely set a boundary for your personal needs, leaving the relationship on positive terms.

4. Time Management: Schedule Wisely

Effective time management can prevent overcommitment by allowing you to allocate your time more strategically.

Action Step: Use a planner to block off time for essential tasks and personal self-care. Include buffer time between commitments to account for unexpected events or downtime.

5. Embrace the Power of "No": Embracing Boundaries

Learning to say No is a crucial skill in breaking the cycle of overcommitment. It's essential to say No sometimes, but more than that, it's about saying Yes to the things that truly matter, fostering a life filled with purpose, connection, and joy.

Breaking the cycle of overcommitment requires intentional effort and a commitment to self-awareness, prioritization, and setting boundaries. By embracing these strategies, you can create a more balanced life that honors your needs and values.

Breaking the Cycle of Overcommitment: Wisdom Notes

Focusing on What Matters

The Vedic texts suggest the importance of discernment (*Viveka*)—the ability to distinguish between what is essential and what is trivial. For instance, in the Bhagavad Gita, Krishna advises Arjuna to focus on his duty as a warrior, highlighting the importance of prioritizing one's responsibilities over distractions.

Example: Consider the story of Guru Nanak, the founder of Sikhism, who often emphasized the importance of selfless service while also advocating for personal balance. He demonstrated that true service arises from a place of inner peace, not from a sense of obligation or overwhelm.

The Importance of Viveka (Discernment)

Viveka, or discernment, is the ability to differentiate between what is truly important and what is not. This skill is crucial in identifying which commitments deserve our time and energy.

Example: The teachings of the sage Adi Shankaracharya emphasize the practice of discernment in spiritual pursuits. He advocated for a life focused on attaining liberation (*Moksha*) over worldly distractions, guiding followers to commit only to endeavors that advance their spiritual growth. Shankaracharya teaches that discernment is not merely an abstract concept but should be applied in everyday decisions. He advises individuals to assess their choices based on their alignment with spiritual growth rather than temporary pleasures.

WISDOM: Four Aids to Discrimination (Sadhana Chatushtaya)

Qualities for Discernment: In "Vivekachudamani," he outlines four essential qualities:

- **Sama**: Calmness of mind. Sama refers to mental tranquility and equanimity. It involves achieving a state of inner peace, free from disturbances caused by external circumstances or internal thoughts. A calm mind is crucial for effective discernment. When the mind is agitated, it can cloud judgment and lead to impulsive decisions. Cultivating calmness allows seekers to reflect deeply and perceive the true nature of reality without distractions.

- **Dama**: Control of the senses. Dama is the ability to control the senses and not be swayed by external stimuli. It involves moderation and restraint in sensory experiences, ensuring that one does not become overly attached to pleasures or distractions. By mastering the senses, individuals can focus their energy on spiritual pursuits rather than being caught up in the transient pleasures of the material world. This control helps in maintaining clarity and discipline, essential for true discernment.

- **Uparati**: Withdrawal from worldly distractions. Uparati involves a conscious withdrawal from activities and distractions that do not contribute to spiritual growth. It means prioritizing inner exploration over external engagements. By reducing distractions, seekers can deepen their contemplation and develop a clearer understanding of their inner selves and the nature of reality.

- **Titiksha**: Endurance of hardships. Titiksha is the ability to endure difficulties, challenges, and discomforts without losing composure or becoming despondent. It reflects resilience and perseverance in the face of obstacles.

- **Teachings**: These qualities help cultivate the inner environment necessary for discernment and spiritual practice.

Christian Perspectives: The Importance of Rest

Christian teachings emphasize the value of rest and reflection. The concept of Sabbath in the Bible encourages individuals to take time off from work and commitments to recharge, reminding us that rest is essential for spiritual and physical well-being.

Research supports the idea that regular periods of rest can improve physical health, reduce stress, and enhance overall well-being. The Sabbath provides a structured time to step back from the demands of life, which can lead to better mental health. Taking time to rest is also viewed as an act of worship. It acknowledges God's sovereignty and provision, reminding believers to trust in God's plans rather than relying solely on their efforts.

The Trap of Bully-Proofing Your Life

The Bully Influence Trap

"No one deserves to be bullied. Everyone has the right to feel safe."

Experiencing bullying is like having a small stone in your shoe. It may seem minor at first, but over time, it causes significant discomfort and pain, distracting you from walking your path.

Understanding the Trap

In the intricate realm of social interactions, few experiences are as painful as bullying. Whether it occurs in classrooms, workplaces, families, or online spaces, its lasting impact can profoundly affect an individual's emotional well-being. To shield themselves from this distressing reality, many people resort to complex strategies aimed at avoiding victimization, such as changing their behavior or withdrawing from social situations. However, these defensive tactics can inadvertently lead to a state of hyper-vigilance, where individuals become excessively cautious and anxious about their interactions. This heightened awareness often results in social isolation, preventing the development of authentic connections and resilience. Rather than creating a sense of safety and belonging, these approaches can entrap individuals, stunting personal growth and hindering their ability to form meaningful relationships.

People bully for a range of reasons, often rooted in complex social, psychological, and environmental factors.

Delving a bit deeper

- **Insecurity and Low Self-Esteem**: Bullies may feel highly insecure and attempt to raise their own status by belittling others, using this masking behavior as a way to compensate for their feelings of inadequacy. Much like a house built on shaky ground, bullies often feel insecure within themselves. **Insecurity and low self-esteem significantly motivate bullying behavior.** Individuals may bully to compensate for feelings of inadequacy, seeking validation from peers by belittling others. This behavior often serves as a projection of their internal struggles, where those who feel weak attempt to exert control to mask their vulnerabilities. Fear of rejection can also drive them to assert dominance preemptively. Additionally, many bullies have experienced bullying themselves or witnessed it, perpetuating a cycle of insecurity. Understanding these motivations can help create environments that foster confidence and positive self-worth, ultimately reducing bullying.

- **Desire for Control or Power**: Some individuals seek to dominate others to gain a sense of power. Bullying provides a temporary boost to their self-worth to boost their ego. **Just as a puppet master pulls strings to control their puppets, some individuals bully to dominate others and establish a sense of power.** This need for control can provide a temporary boost to their self-worth. For example, a manager who feels threatened by a talented employee might undermine them to feel more secure in their position.

- **Social Dynamics**: Bullying frequently occurs in group settings, where peer pressure influences behavior. Bullying can also happen in the family system where interference of other relatives is high. **Some may engage in bullying to fit in or gain acceptance from a specific group. For instance, a teenager might join in teasing a classmate simply to be accepted by their friends, even if they don't personally agree with the behavior.** Similarly, a family member might join others to tease a new member in the house or family setting just to gain acceptance.

- **Learned Behavior**: Individuals who experience or witness bullying—whether at home, in school, or through media—may imitate these actions, believing they are acceptable ways to interact with others. *For example, a* *child who sees older siblings, parents, relatives, peers or grandparents bullying might see it as a normal way to interact with peers, friends, partner or other family members.*

- **Lack of Empathy**: Some bullies struggle to empathize with their victims, making it easier for them to inflict harm without understanding the emotional impact of their actions. For instance, a person might make hurtful comments online, failing to realize the pain it causes to the recipient.

- **Coping Mechanism**: Bullying can act as a misguided distraction, similar to a person using a hammer to fix a delicate clock. *When faced with personal stress or issues, some individuals may target others to temporarily divert attention from their own problems.* For example, someone dealing with family issues might bully a classmate as a way to cope with their feelings of powerlessness.

- **Attention-Seeking**: Just as a performer craves the spotlight, some bullies seek attention, even if it's negative. Bullying can also be a means to gain attention, even if it's negative. The reactions of others can reinforce this behavior, making it more appealing. *Attention-seeking behavior is a significant motivator behind bullying, as individuals often act out to gain visibility, even if it's negative. This desire for attention can lead to a cycle of reinforcement, where reactions from peers validate and encourage further bullying.* In group settings, bullies may be viewed as dominant, creating pressure for others to join in or remain silent. Additionally, attention-seeking can mask deeper emotional struggles; for instance, a child facing difficulties at home might bully to distract from their vulnerabilities. Ultimately, the need to compete for attention among peers can drive individuals to harmful behaviors. Recognizing this motivation can help address root causes and promote healthier ways for people to seek acknowledgment and connection.

- **Cultural and Environmental Factors**: Cultural and environmental factors play a significant role in shaping behaviors, including bullying. *Just as weeds thrive in an untended garden, environments that tolerate aggression can cultivate a culture where bullying becomes normalized.* In families where aggression is overlooked or even encouraged, children may learn that bullying is an acceptable form of interaction. In school settings, the pressure to conform can lead to the normalization of bullying behaviors. If a group of friends engages in teasing or exclusion, others may feel obligated to join in to maintain their social standing. This can create an environment where bullying is not only tolerated but expected, further entrenching harmful behaviors. In professional environments, a culture that values competitiveness over collaboration can breed bullying. When aggressive behavior is overlooked or rewarded—such as in high-stakes sales environments—employees may resort to bullying to assert dominance or achieve success. This fosters a toxic atmosphere that impacts everyone's well-being.

- **Social Isolation**: By bullying, they want to isolate the victim. The victim suffers from loneliness and a lack of support, which are crucial for emotional well-being. This way, the bully tries to feel superior.

Bullies Have Two Faces

The concept of bullies having "two faces" refers to the duality in their behavior and personality. This duality can manifest in several ways:

- **Public Persona vs. Private Behavior**: Many bullies maintain a charming or likable facade in public, presenting themselves as friendly or charismatic. However, in private or among targeted individuals, they exhibit aggressive or hurtful behavior. This contrast can confuse victims and make it difficult for others to believe the bullying is happening.

- **Chameleon-Like Adaptability**: Bullies can adapt their behavior based on their audience. In front of authority figures, they may act respectful and compliant, while in peer settings, they switch to aggressive or dismissive behavior. This adaptability allows them to evade accountability and maintain a positive image.

- **Victim vs. Aggressor:** Some bullies may portray themselves as victims in certain situations, deflecting blame and manipulating others' perceptions. By positioning themselves as misunderstood or unfairly treated, they can garner sympathy while continuing their harmful actions behind the scenes.

How to Come Out of the Trap of Bullies

Dealing with bullies can be challenging, but there are effective strategies to address the situation:

- **Stay Composed**: Try to keep your cool when faced with a bully. Reacting with anger or fear can escalate their behavior. Take deep breaths and stay calm.

- **Be Assertive**: Use confident body language and speak firmly. Let the bully know their behavior is unacceptable with statements like, "I don't appreciate that." *Example*: If a friend constantly makes fun of you, say, "I don't appreciate those jokes. I'd like you to stop."

- **Limit Contact:** If interactions with a certain family member or in a new setting consistently lead to negativity, consider limiting your time with them. Protecting your mental well-being is essential.

- *Example:* If family gatherings become overwhelming, plan to attend fewer events or take breaks during gatherings.

- **Document Incidents**: Keep a detailed record of bullying episodes, noting the date, time, and specifics of what happened. This can be helpful if you decide to report the bullying.

- **Seek Support**: Talk to trusted friends, family, or mentors about what you're experiencing. Having a support network can make you feel less alone and more empowered.

- **Report the Behavior**: If bullying continues, don't hesitate to inform a teacher, supervisor, friend or HR representative.

- **Prioritize Self-Care**: Engage in activities that uplift your mood and boost your self-esteem, such as hobbies, exercise, or mindfulness. Taking care of your mental health is vital.

- **Avoid Retaliation**: While it might be tempting to retaliate, responding with aggression can escalate the situation. Focus on constructive responses instead of seeking revenge. *Example*: If someone spreads rumors about you, resist the urge to retaliate. Instead, focus on building positive relationships with others.

- **Know When to Walk Away**: Sometimes, the best option is to disengage. If possible, remove yourself from the environment where bullying occurs and seek out more supportive spaces. Keep your boundaries intact. Just as you protect a home by building walls, protect your mind.

- **Empower Yourself and Others**: Stand up for yourself and support others who are being bullied. Creating a culture of kindness can help reduce bullying overall.

- *Example*: If you see someone being teased, intervene by saying, "That's not right. Let's include everyone." This encourages a supportive environment.

- **Situation**: You hear someone gossiping or spreading rumors about another person.

- **Response**: "I don't think it's fair to talk about someone when they're not here. Let's keep the conversation respectful."

- **Situation**: A group is mocking someone for their appearance or habits.

- **Response**: "That's not funny. We should appreciate people for who they are, not tear them down."

- **Situation**: You come across a hurtful comment or post on social media aimed at someone.

- **Response**: "This isn't right. We need to be more mindful and kind in what we share online."

"In a world where you can be anything, be kind."

The Trap of Not Taking Control of Your Life

The Savior Trap

The biggest trap of life is to hand over the control of your life to someone in the name of love, attachment or relationship.

Relying too much on other people makes you indecisive or following a path that has been chalked down by others for you. Where is your identity? In our quest for connection and belonging, we often find ourselves caught in the "Savior Trap." This phenomenon occurs when we willingly relinquish control of our lives to others, believing that love or attachment justifies such surrender. *While it may feel noble to prioritize someone else's needs over our own, this trap can lead to a loss of identity, resentment, and ultimately, a sense of powerlessness.*

If you rely too much on others, they have control over your life, and sometimes you might feel lost.

This dual trap involves waiting for someone else to rescue you from life's challenges or attempting to change others according to your expectations. Both approaches can lead to disappointment and frustration. You have to catch your own dreams and ask someone else to take that leap of faith or follow your dreams.

To overcome this trap, recognize that personal empowerment is the key to your own success. Take control of your life and actively work toward your goals. When it comes to relationships, accept people for who they are rather than trying to mold them into your idealized version. Healthy relationships are built on acceptance and support, not unrealistic expectations.

The Allure of Sacrifice

Sacrificing your needs for loved ones can seem noble. **"The greatest gift of life is friendship,"** said Hubert H. Humphrey, but this gift can quickly become a burden if it demands your own well-being. *We are conditioned to believe that love means putting others first. For instance, consider a woman who constantly prioritizes her partner's needs, neglecting her own passions.* She may tell herself that her sacrifices are acts of love, yet over time, she may feel unfulfilled and resentful. This dynamic is like a flower wilting in the shade of another plant, losing its chance to thrive.

The Slippery Slope of Dependency

The Savior Trap is insidious. Initially, it may feel rewarding to support someone, especially if that person is going through a difficult time. However, as time goes on, this support can shift into dependency. The individual being "saved" may become reliant on their partner for emotional stability, while the savior feels obligated to maintain that support at all costs.

Imagine a man who devotes himself entirely to caring for his friend, who struggles with addiction. While his intentions are good, he might find that he's sacrificing his own mental health, passions, and friendships.

The Consequences of Inaction

When we don't assert control over our lives, we may inadvertently hand the reins to those around us. **Eleanor Roosevelt** famously said, **"No one can make you feel inferior without your consent."** This highlights the importance of self-agency. By allowing others to dictate our choices, we give away our power and, over time, may come to resent those we feel have taken control.

The Cost of Identity Loss

One of the profound impacts of the Savior Trap is the erosion of self-identity. True connection thrives when two souls meet, but each remains anchored in their own identity. To lose yourself in another is to lose the very essence that makes you whole. When individuals invest all their energy into caring for others, they often forget who they are outside that relationship. Hobbies, ambitions, and personal goals take a backseat, leading to a sense of emptiness.

Reclaiming one's identity after experiencing the Savior Trap can be a challenging journey. It often requires conscious effort to rediscover lost passions and redefine personal goals. Like a garden that has been overtaken by weeds, it takes time and diligence to clear the space for one's own growth again.

Consider Lina, who, after years of prioritizing her partner's career over her own, finally recognized the toll it had taken on her identity. She began to set aside time each week for herself—initially just an hour to read, then eventually dedicating weekends to her love for hiking. With every step on the trail, she felt more connected to herself, rediscovering the joy that had been overshadowed for so long. Gradually, Lina began to cultivate her own dreams again, taking art classes and reconnecting with friends.

Things on Which You Can Exercise Control

The aspects over which you have control in your life include your reactions, decisions, attitudes, and the boundaries set by you.

1. Reactions: Your reactions should not be based on biases or opinions of other people. They are your reaction for a reason. Make proper judgments, use your brain. **If you let anyone else influence you, your reaction is actually a reflection of their judgment and opinion.** Be aware! You gave the control over to someone else's hand. Take back your power.

2. Decisions: Your decisions indicate your direction. **Your instinct should show you a direction in your life matters.** You have to be confident and assertive. For that, you should make sure that your decision is loud and clear to other people and you stand by its implications. *You can drive your car, so why let anyone else take control over the steering wheel and steer you*

toward where they want you to go. You absolutely have the power to think for yourself. You definitely have the know-how to reach a conclusion. Use your intuition as deep innate inner knowledge that is composed of data that your brain has observed over the course of your life. When used wisely, it can be an incredible source to guide you to make important decisions. Learn to quiet your mind, develop a greater awareness of what you're thinking and feeling, and listen to your body.

People who have no boundaries often accommodate others before themselves.

If the people around you are always doing or saying things that frustrate you to your core, you have to put your foot down. People will never know what they're

Breaking Free from the Trap

Escaping the Savior Trap requires conscious effort and spiritual guidance. Both the Bible and the Bhagavad Gita provide wisdom that can help individuals reclaim their identities and find balance in their relationships.

1. Recognizing Your Worth

The journey begins with recognizing your inherent value. In the Bible, **Psalm 139:14** states, "I praise you because I am fearfully and wonderfully made; your works are wonderful, I know that full well." This verse reminds us that each person is unique and valuable in their own right. Embracing this truth is essential in breaking free from the trap of self-neglect. The first step in breaking free is to recognize your inherent worth. The **Guru Granth Sahib** reminds us that **"You are part of the Infinite" (Ang 24)**, highlighting our divine nature and value. Understanding that you are worthy of love and respect is essential in reclaiming your identity. The Guru Granth Sahib teaches us the importance of self-awareness and humility. In **Ang 24**, it states, **"Recognize the Divine within yourself, for you are part of the Infinite."** This affirmation encourages us to see ourselves as valuable and deserving of love, fostering a sense of self-worth that isn't dependent on others.

2. Set Boundaries

Establish clear boundaries to protect your emotional well-being. **"Good fences make good neighbors,"** as Robert Frost said. Communicate openly about what you can give.

3. Prioritize Self-Care

Make self-care a non-negotiable part of your routine. As the airline safety briefing reminds us, **"Put on your own oxygen mask before assisting others."** Prioritizing your own needs ensures you have the energy to support others without losing yourself. *Example*: Schedule regular "me time" for activities that rejuvenate you, like reading, exercising, or pursuing a hobby.

4. Cultivating Independence

Encouraging independence in others is a vital part of breaking free from the Savior Trap. The Bible speaks to the importance of wisdom in **Proverbs 3:5-6**: "Trust in the Lord with all your heart and lean not on your own understanding; in all your ways submit to him, and he will make your paths straight." This suggests that guiding others to seek their own paths can lead to greater wisdom and fulfillment. The Guru Granth Sahib emphasizes the importance of self-reliance. In **Ang 74**, it says, **"The true teacher shows the way; he does not do the work for you."** This encourages us to guide others while empowering them to take charge of their own lives.

5. Seeking Spiritual Guidance

The Gita emphasizes the importance of surrendering to the divine. In **Chapter 18, Verse 66**, Lord Krishna advises, **"Abandon all varieties of religion and just surrender unto Me. I shall deliver you from all sinful reactions. Do not fear**."This call to surrender encourages individuals to trust in a higher power, providing comfort and direction in times of uncertainty. The Guru Granth Sahib emphasizes the importance of connection with the Divine. In **Ang 61**, it states, **"With the Guru's grace, one attains peace."** This highlights the power of spiritual insight in overcoming personal struggles. Seek His grace always.

Breaking free from the Savior Trap is a transformative journey of self-discovery, empowerment, and spiritual growth. By recognizing your inner value, establishing healthy boundaries, prioritizing self-care, encouraging independence, and seeking spiritual guidance, you can reclaim your identity and nurture healthier relationships.

If you don't take control of your life, someone else will inevitably step in to fill that void. The journey to reclaiming your identity is essential for living authentically. As **Friedrich Nietzsche** aptly noted, **"He who has a why to live can bear almost any how."** Finding your "why"—your passion and purpose—is crucial in navigating life's challenges.

By recognizing your value, establishing boundaries, empowering those around you, and seeking guidance, you can take charge of your life and honor your unique journey. Embrace the wisdom of those who came before you and step boldly into the life you deserve.

The Trap of Not Comprehending What You're Capable Of

The Seriousness Trap

"Often, the greatest trap we face is not the obstacles around us, but the limits we place on ourselves; true freedom lies in recognizing our boundless potential."

One of the most profound and pervasive mistakes people make is failing to believe in their own capabilities. This fundamental lapse in self-belief can stifle potential, limit opportunities, and undermine personal growth. When individuals do not recognize their own strengths and possibilities, they effectively constrain their own success and happiness. In a world brimming with potential, the most intricate prison is often the one we build within our own minds. It's a cage forged from self-doubt, shaped by past failures, and painted over with the societal expectations we internalize. Let's explore how this trap can ensnare us and, more importantly, how to break free.

The Mirage of Limitations

Imagine standing at the edge of a vast canyon, a chasm that seems insurmountable. On one side, you see all your dreams and aspirations, glimmering like distant stars. On the other, the solid ground of your current reality, familiar but confining. Many people, when faced with this divide, mistakenly believe they are incapable of crossing it. This illusion creates a mirage of limitations that clouds their vision.

The stories we tell ourselves often reinforce these barriers. "I'm not good enough," "I've failed before," or "That's not for people like me." Each thought adds another layer to the wall, making it seem ever more impenetrable. We start to identify with our limitations rather than our potential, and in doing so, we become trapped in a cycle of stagnation.

When people doubt their abilities, they often avoid taking risks or pursuing new opportunities. This hesitation can lead to missed chances for career advancement, personal development, and fulfilling experiences. Believing in one's capabilities is crucial for seizing opportunities that could lead to significant achievements and growth.

Self-doubt can prevent individuals from exploring their full range of talents and interests. When people lack confidence, they may shy away from challenges that could lead to personal and professional growth. This reluctance to step outside their comfort zone means they never fully discover or develop their potential.

Reduced Performance

- **Self-Fulfilling Prophecy:** Believing that one is incapable can become a self-fulfilling prophecy. If individuals doubt their abilities, they may perform below their actual potential due to a lack of effort, motivation, or resilience. This diminished performance can further reinforce their self-doubt, creating a cycle of underachievement.

Strained Relationships

- **Impact on Others:** Self-doubt can also affect interpersonal relationships. When people lack confidence, they might not assert themselves effectively or engage in meaningful ways. This can lead to misunderstandings, missed collaborations, and strained relationships, impacting both personal and professional spheres.

Beyond the Trap
The Power of Perspective

However, the first step toward liberation is recognizing that limitations are often self-imposed. This realization can be transformative. By reframing our perspectives, we can begin to dismantle the walls we've built.

Consider the concept of the growth mindset, popularized by psychologist Carol Dweck. It encourages us to view challenges as opportunities for learning rather than insurmountable obstacles. With this mindset, every failure is not a reflection of our abilities but a stepping stone towards growth. It's through setbacks that you learn, adapt, and build the resilience needed for success.

To shift your perspective, start by examining your beliefs. Ask yourself:

- What narratives am I telling myself?
- Where do these beliefs originate?
- What evidence contradicts these narratives?

You might discover that many of your perceived limitations are based on outdated stories or external voices that you've absorbed over the years.

The Role of Fear

Fear often plays a pivotal role in keeping us trapped. ***Fear of failure, fear of judgment, and fear of the unknown*** can paralyze even the most talented individuals. It whispers insidious thoughts, convincing us that staying in our comfort zones is safer than venturing into the unfamiliar.

Yet, what is the cost of this fear? It may shield us from immediate discomfort, but it also robs us of our potential. **Think of fear as a shadow; it grows larger the closer we get to confronting it.** When we take that step forward—no matter how small—the shadow diminishes, revealing the light of possibility.

Cultivating Courage

To combat fear, we must cultivate courage. Courage is not the absence of fear, but the ability to act in spite of it. This requires practice and self-compassion. Start with small, manageable challenges that push you slightly beyond your comfort zone. Each small victory will build your confidence and help you recognize your capabilities.

Consider journaling your experiences. Reflect on moments when you stepped outside your comfort zone. What did you learn? How did you feel? Over time, these reflections will serve as a powerful reminder of your strength and resilience.

The Journey of Self-Discovery

Ultimately, comprehending what you're capable of is a journey of self-discovery. *It involves peeling back the layers of doubt and fear to uncover the potential that lies within.* This process is not linear; it's a winding path with setbacks and triumphs. Embrace the journey, and remember that every step forward, no matter how small, brings you closer to your true self.

As you move forward, keep this in mind: you are capable of more than you know. The limitations you perceive are often far less than the possibilities that await you. So, take a deep breath, step into the unknown, and let your potential unfold.

"The boundaries you place on yourself are often illusions. Step beyond them, and you'll discover a world of untapped possibilities waiting to be explored."

Here are some strategies to help individuals overcome self-doubt and recognize their true potential:

1. **Acknowledge and Reflect**

   - **Identify Strengths:** Take time to reflect on past successes and strengths. Acknowledging what you have already achieved can help reinforce your self-belief.

- ○ **Journal Achievements:** Keeping a record of accomplishments and positive feedback can serve as a tangible reminder of your capabilities.

2. **Challenge Negative Thoughts**

   - ○ **Reframe Doubts:** Actively challenge and reframe negative thoughts. Cognitive restructuring can help shift your perspective from self-doubt to self-empowerment.

   - ○ **Affirmations:** Use positive affirmations to counteract negative self-talk and build confidence.

3. **Set and Achieve Goals**

   - ○ **Small Steps:** Break down larger goals into smaller, manageable tasks. Achieving these incremental goals can build confidence and momentum.

   - ○ **Celebrate Progress:** Recognize and celebrate progress, no matter how small. Celebrating milestones can reinforce a sense of accomplishment and capability.

4. **Embrace Learning and Growth**

   - ○ **View Failure as Learning:** Treat failures and setbacks as opportunities for learning and growth rather than reflections of inadequacy.

   - ○ **Adopt a Growth Mindset:** Embrace a growth mindset that values effort, learning, and perseverance over innate talent or immediate success.

5. **Practice Self-Compassion**

   - ○ **Be Kind to Yourself:** Practice self-compassion and treat yourself with the same kindness and understanding that you would offer to a friend.

   - ○ **Forgive Mistakes:** Understand that mistakes and imperfections are part of the learning process and do not define your worth or capabilities.

Always Believe in the Ripple Effect of Belief: Dare to Believe

Believing in one's own capabilities is not just about achieving success; it is about unlocking potential, fostering resilience, and living a fulfilling life. When individuals recognize and embrace their abilities, they open doors to new possibilities and contribute meaningfully to their own lives and the world around them. The power of belief extends beyond individual experiences. When people believe in themselves, they not only enhance their own lives but also positively impact those around them. This ripple effect can lead to a more supportive and optimistic community, where collective belief fosters shared success and growth.

The Seed of Potential Story: Beautiful story of Anya

In a quiet village, there lived a young girl named Anya. Known for her gentle spirit, she often felt invisible among her boisterous classmates, preferring to sit under the old oak tree with a book rather than join in their games. Deep down, Anya dreamed of becoming a writer, but self-doubt gnawed at her. "I'm not good enough," she whispered to herself, convinced her stories would never be as captivating as those of her favorite authors.

One rainy afternoon, while exploring the attic of her grandmother's house, Anya stumbled upon an old, dusty journal. Intrigued, she carefully opened it to find her grandmother's stories—tales of adventure, love, and resilience. Each page was filled with vibrant imagery and heartfelt emotion, transporting Anya to distant lands and moments of triumph.

As she read, a spark ignited within her. Inspired, Anya grabbed her own notebook and began to write. Words flowed from her pen like a rushing river, capturing her thoughts and dreams. But as days passed, doubt crept back in. "What if no one likes my story?" she fretted, her confidence waning.

Then one evening, as she was about to close her journal in defeat, she remembered her grandmother's words: "Every seed has the potential to grow into something beautiful." Those words echoed in her mind, stirring something deep within her.

The Decision

With renewed determination, Anya decided to share her story at the upcoming village fair, a place where the community gathered to celebrate local talents. Nervously, she prepared herself, rehearsing her story in front of her mirror, envisioning the joy her words could bring.

On the day of the fair, the sun shone brightly, and the village square buzzed with excitement. Anya stood backstage, her heart racing as she clutched her journal tightly. She could hear laughter and chatter from the crowd, and for a moment, doubt washed over her again. "What if I fail?"

But then she thought of her grandmother and the stories that had inspired her. Taking a deep breath, Anya stepped onto the small stage, her legs trembling. She looked out at the faces before her—friends, neighbors, and familiar smiles encouraging her to begin.

The Performance

As Anya opened her journal and began to read, her voice trembled at first, but then it grew stronger. She painted vivid scenes of adventure and friendship, weaving her characters into the fabric of her own dreams. The audience leaned in, captivated by her words, their eyes shining with connection and understanding.

With each paragraph, Anya felt a wave of confidence wash over her. Laughter and gasps punctuated her reading, and she could see her audience visualizing the world she had created. When she finished, the square erupted in applause, a sound that resonated deep within her heart.

Tears of joy filled her eyes as she realized the truth: her voice mattered. In that moment, she understood that the seed of potential within her had begun to bloom. Anya stepped off the stage, embraced by friends who congratulated her and encouraged her to keep writing.

The Transformation

From that day on, Anya embraced her identity as a writer. She started a blog to share her stories, connecting with people beyond her village. The more she wrote, the more her confidence grew. Each story was a reminder of her grandmother's wisdom – that she had the power to create beauty and inspire others.

Years later, Anya published her first book, filled with the tales of adventure and imagination that had once lived only in her heart. At her book launch, she stood before a crowd of eager readers, just as she had at the fair, but this time she felt a profound sense of belonging.

Conclusion

Anya's journey teaches us that often, the greatest obstacles we face are the doubts we hold within ourselves. By nurturing our potential and sharing our unique gifts, we can inspire others and discover the beauty that lies within us. Like a seed that grows into a towering tree, our true capabilities can flourish when we dare to believe in ourselves.

The Spiritual Essence of Self-Belief

In the vast and intricate tapestry of existence, self-belief emerges as a sacred thread that weaves together our spiritual journey with our earthly experience. At its core, self-belief is not merely an act of personal confidence but a profound acknowledgment of the divine essence within us. It is an acknowledgment that we are co-creators of our reality, endowed with infinite potential and a connection to a higher source.

The Divine Spark Within: Wisdom Notes

Every soul carries a divine spark, a piece of the Universe's boundless energy. Self-belief is an expression of recognizing and embracing this inner light. When we believe in ourselves, we are affirming our connection to the divine and our role in manifesting our highest potential. This belief is a spiritual affirmation that we are worthy of love, abundance, and fulfillment, simply by virtue of our existence.

"In the heart of every being lies a lamp,

Ignite it with your faith and love.

The world outside may be dark,

But the light within will guide you above."

Nurturing the Divine Essence - To nurture the divine essence within the mind, Gurbani emphasizes the importance of spiritual practices such as Nitnem (Meditation and Reading in the morning, evening, and night hymns), Sahaj Paath (Reading a few pages of Shri Guru Granth Sahib ji), Reflections on Gurbani Shabads, Living life as per the tenets of Sikhi, and recitation of the sacred Naam (Divine Name). These practices allow us to dive into the depths of our consciousness, quieting the mind and aligning it with the divine light within.

Through meditation, we learn to observe our thoughts and emotions that arise within us without judgment and attachment. This practice helps us detach from the transient aspects of the mind and connect with the unchanging divinity that resides within us.

Recitation of Naam is a powerful tool to rekindle our awareness of the divine essence within. By repeating the sacred Name, we invoke the presence of the Divine and establish a deep connection with our true nature.

Aligning with Divine Purpose

Belief in oneself is a sacred alignment with one's divine purpose. It is an act of trust in the path laid out for us by the Universe or a higher power. When we embrace self-belief, we align our actions and intentions with our spiritual purpose, allowing us to flow with the currents of our true calling. This alignment fosters a deeper sense of meaning and fulfillment, as we recognize that our efforts and aspirations are part of a greater cosmic plan.

The Power of Intention

In spiritual traditions, intention is seen as a powerful force that shapes reality. Self-belief is intrinsically linked to the power of intention. When we believe in our capabilities, we set intentions that resonate with our highest good and the greater good. Our thoughts, actions, and desires become harmonized with the Universe's vibrations, enabling us to attract and manifest the experiences and opportunities that align with our spiritual goals.

Faith in the Unseen

Self-belief requires faith in the unseen and the unknown. It is a spiritual practice of trusting in the process, even when the outcomes are not immediately visible. Just as faith in a higher power or the Universe requires surrender and trust, so too does self-belief demand that we trust in our own inherent capabilities and potential. This faith helps us navigate uncertainty and embrace the journey with grace and courage.

Quote from Sai Baba:

"The one who has faith is never lost; the one who surrenders to the divine will find their way."

Short Reflection

Sai Baba's teachings remind us that the journey to discovering our potential begins with faith—faith in ourselves, in the divine, and in the interconnectedness of all beings. By looking within, serving others, and maintaining patience, we can unlock the greatness that resides in each of us.

The Trap of Taking Life Too Seriously

The Seriousness Trap

Focusing too much on responsibilities and not enough on joy, fun, or spontaneity can lead to regrets about not fully enjoying life.

> "Life is a delicate balance; when we focus too much on our responsibilities, we forget to dance in the rain. Embrace joy, for it is the thread that weaves a tapestry of fulfillment."

Life, with its myriad responsibilities, challenges, and uncertainties, can sometimes feel overwhelmingly serious. The pursuit of success, the desire to meet societal expectations, and the fear of failure can lead you to adopt an overly serious approach to life. While a certain level of seriousness is fine and necessary for achieving goals and managing responsibilities, an excessive focus on it can lead to stress, burnout, and a diminished quality of life. Some people believe that success and happiness come solely from hard work and seriousness, misunderstanding the role of relaxation, joy, and balance in a fulfilling life.

Impact: This belief can lead to a life focused on achievements and seriousness, rather than on experiences that truly bring happiness and contentment.

When you start to prioritize work, responsibilities, and achievements above all else, you will start neglecting essential aspects of well-being, such as relaxation, leisure, and self-care. Over time, this imbalance can lead to physical and mental health issues. It will eat you slowly. **Life will go by, and you will regret you could not enjoy the little things in life. In the relentless pursuit**

of perfection and success, you will sacrifice joy and spontaneity. What is life anyway without joy?

Here are some examples of how people might take life too seriously, highlighting the potential consequences:

1. **Obsessing Over Career Success**

    o   **Example:** A person might spend all their time working, even on weekends and holidays, to climb the corporate ladder. They may sacrifice time with family, miss important events, and neglect their health in the pursuit of career success.

    o   **Consequence:** This can lead to burnout, strained relationships, and a lack of fulfillment, as they miss out on other important aspects of life.

2. **Overplanning and Control**

    o   **Example:** Someone might plan every detail of their day, from meals to activities, leaving no room for spontaneity. If things don't go according to plan, they become stressed and anxious.

    o   **Consequence:** This rigid approach can prevent them from enjoying unexpected opportunities or simple pleasures, making life feel more like a chore than an adventure.

3. **Overcommitment to Social or Family Obligations**

    o   **Example:** A person might feel obligated to attend every family gathering, social event, or volunteer opportunity, even when they're exhausted or have other priorities.

    o   **Consequence:** This over-commitment can lead to stress, resentment, and a lack of personal time for relaxation or pursuing individual interests.

4. **Taking Relationships Too Seriously**

    o   **Example:** A person might be overly critical or controlling in their relationships, insisting on everything being perfect and expecting their partner or friends to meet unrealistic standards.

○ **Consequence:** This can strain relationships, leading to conflicts, misunderstandings, and possibly the loss of meaningful connections.

To avoid the pitfalls of taking life too seriously, it is essential to cultivate a more balanced approach that prioritizes joy, spontaneity, and self-compassion. One of the first steps in achieving this balance is to embrace imperfection. Beauty often lies in the imperfect—the quirks, the scars, the unexpected. By embracing these aspects of ourselves, we can appreciate the true beauty of life.

Lack of Spontaneity

- **Problem:** Sticking rigidly to plans and routines can leave little room for spontaneity or unexpected pleasures.

- **Impact:** It can lead to a life that feels overly controlled and predictable, with fewer moments of excitement or adventure.

Spontaneity is also an important aspect of living a balanced life. Being open to new experiences and allowing room for flexibility in daily routines can add excitement and variety to life. Whether it's taking an impromptu trip, trying a new hobby, or simply breaking away from a daily routine, spontaneity can invigorate the spirit and foster a sense of adventure in you. It can also help you break free from the monotony of a highly structured life and create opportunities for personal growth and connection with others.

Story of Yuvan: The Weight of Responsibility

In the bustling city of New York, where skyscrapers kissed the clouds and life moved at a frenetic pace, lived a man named Yuvan. Known for his diligence and commitment, he was the embodiment of responsibility. He worked long hours as an accountant, tirelessly crunching numbers to ensure his clients' financial well-being. While his colleagues enjoyed their lunch breaks and shared laughter, Yuvan often stayed at his desk, buried in spreadsheets and reports.

As the days turned into weeks, and weeks into years, he became more consumed by his work. His friends would invite him out for drinks or a weekend getaway, but he always had an excuse. "I can't; I have to finish this project," he'd say, his voice tinged with a hint of pride. After all, he thought, who else would take care of the important tasks?

The Catalyst

One evening, while organizing his office, Yuvan stumbled upon an old photo album. Curiosity piqued, he opened it to find images of his younger self, full of laughter and spontaneity. There he was, hiking in the mountains with friends, dancing at parties, and even attempting to paint. Each photo radiated joy, a stark contrast to the rigid life he now led.

A wave of nostalgia washed over him, and for the first time in years, he felt a pang of regret. "When did I stop having fun?" he wondered. The realization hit him hard – he had allowed responsibilities to overshadow the vibrant experiences that once defined him.

A Moment of Reckoning

Determined to change, Yuvan decided to attend a local art class that weekend. He had always enjoyed painting, but the demands of adulthood had pushed it aside. As he stepped into the studio, a mix of excitement and nervousness washed over him. The room was filled with laughter and creativity, a stark contrast to his sterile office environment.

That day, he picked up a brush and let his imagination flow. Colors splashed across the canvas, and with each stroke, he felt a weight lift from his shoulders. For the first time in a long while, he was present—fully engaged in the moment. Laughter bubbled around him as he connected with fellow artists, sharing stories and laughter over their shared love for creativity.

Embracing Joy

Over the following weeks, Yuvan made a conscious effort to embrace spontaneity. He began saying yes to invitations, whether it was joining friends for a spontaneous road trip or simply enjoying a quiet evening in the park. Each experience filled him with a sense of joy he had long forgotten.

His coworkers noticed a change as well. He smiled more, laughed louder, and even organized a team outing. They went bowling one Friday night, where he embraced the playful side of life. He was no longer just the responsible accountant; he was a friend, a teammate, and a source of laughter.

The Balance

As the seasons changed, so did Yuvan's outlook on life. He learned to balance his responsibilities with moments of joy and spontaneity. He still worked hard, but he also made time for the things that brought him happiness. He realized that life was not just about fulfilling duties; it was about creating memories and savoring the present.

One afternoon, while enjoying a picnic with friends, he paused to soak in the beauty around him – the laughter, the delicious food, and the warmth of the sun. He felt a deep sense of gratitude for the simple moments that brought richness to life.

Conclusion

Yuvan's journey taught him that while responsibilities are essential, they should never overshadow the joy and spontaneity that make life worth living. He had learned to embrace the delicate balance of life, finding fulfillment in both his work and his passions.

As he looked at the horizon, he whispered to himself, "Life is a dance, and I intend to enjoy every step." With this newfound wisdom, he approached each day with a heart full of gratitude, reminding himself to embrace joy, for it was the thread that wove a tapestry of fulfillment in his life.

Some Insights from Different Religious Perspectives

Christianity: Trust in God

- **Teaching:** Christianity encourages believers to trust in God rather than being overly concerned with the worries of the world. Jesus teaches not to be anxious about life, emphasizing the importance of faith and trust in God's provision.

- **Example:** In the Sermon on the Mount, Jesus says, "Therefore I tell you, do not worry about your life, what you will eat or drink; or about your body, what you will wear. Is not life more than food, and the body more than clothes?" (Matthew 6:25).

- **Message:** The teaching suggests that excessive worry and seriousness can distract from the deeper spiritual connection with God and the joy that comes from trusting in His care.

Hinduism: Lila (Divine Play)

- **Teaching:** In Hinduism, the concept of **Lila** refers to life as a divine play, where the Universe and all activities within it are a manifestation of the divine's playfulness.

  - **Example:** The stories of Krishna, who is often depicted as playful and mischievous, embody the idea that life should be approached with a sense of playfulness rather than seriousness.

  - **Message:** This teaching encourages a light-hearted approach to life, recognizing the impermanence and playful nature of existence, urging people not to become overly attached or serious.

Buddhism: The Middle Way

- **Teaching:** Buddhism advocates for the Middle Way, a path of moderation between self-indulgence and self-mortification. This approach encourages avoiding extremes in life, including taking life too seriously.

- **Example:** The Buddha's life itself is an example of this principle. After experiencing both extreme luxury and severe asceticism, he realized that neither extreme brought him enlightenment, leading him to advocate the Middle Way.

- **Message:** By practicing mindfulness and focusing on the present moment, Buddhism teaches that one can avoid the extremes of seriousness and live a balanced, contented life.

Judaism: Simcha (Joy)

- **Teaching:** Judaism places a high value on **Simcha**, or joy, particularly in the service of God. Joy is seen as a vital part of spiritual life, and taking life too seriously can detract from this joy.

- **Example:** The Book of Ecclesiastes (Kohelet) advises, "There is nothing better for a person than to enjoy their work, because that is their lot" (Ecclesiastes 3:22).

- **Message:** This teaching encourages finding joy in everyday life and in one's work, suggesting that a balance between seriousness and joy is essential for a fulfilling life.

Sikhism: Hukam (Divine Will)

- **Teaching:** In Sikhism, **Hukam** refers to the divine will or order, and it is taught that one should live in acceptance of God's will rather than resisting it.

- **Example:** The Guru Granth Sahib, the central religious scripture of Sikhism, teaches, "By Your Will, everything happens; whatever You do comes to pass."

- **Message:** This belief encourages Sikhs to live with a sense of acceptance and trust, rather than taking life too seriously or trying to control every aspect of it.

Across religions, there is a common theme of encouraging a balanced approach to life. Whether through trust in a higher power, finding joy in everyday moments, or practicing moderation, these teachings guide followers to avoid the pitfalls of taking life too seriously. By embracing these spiritual principles, individuals can cultivate a life that is both meaningful and joyful.

Beyond the Trap

- **Embrace Imperfection:** Accept that mistakes are a part of life and can lead to growth.

- **Balance Work and Play:** Make time for fun, relaxation, and activities that bring you joy.

- **Cultivate Spontaneity:** Allow yourself to be flexible and open to new experiences.

- **Practice Mindfulness:** Focus on the present moment and appreciate the simple pleasures in life.

- **Laugh More:** Don't take yourself too seriously—humor and laughter can lighten even the heaviest of burdens.

In life's grand stage,

Don't let joy slip away,

For seriousness steals the brightness of the day.

"जीवन की राह में हंसना भी एक धर्म है,

गंभीरता से दुख बढ़े, हंसना सुख का कर्म है।"

(Translation: In the journey of life, laughter is also a virtue,

Seriousness increases sorrow, while laughter is the essence of joy.)

The Trap of Ignoring the Power of Habits

The Complacency Trap

"Underestimating the power of habits is like ignoring the currents of a river; They shape your course, often without you realizing it."

Ignoring the power of habits is a common mistake that can lead to a lack of direction and achievement in your life. By recognizing the importance of habits and actively working to develop positive ones, you can create a foundation for lasting success and fulfillment. If you fail to establish and maintain positive habits, such as regular exercise, healthy eating, or continuous learning, it can lead to long-term negative consequences. Habits shape daily life and overall success and fulfillment. ***If you do not harness the power of daily habits, it can lead to a life that feels unproductive, chaotic, and unfulfilled.*** Habits are the building blocks of your daily routines and, over time, they shape your character and determine your success. **Positive habits often lead to opportunities, while the lack of them can result in missed chances.** For instance, a habit of networking and continuous learning can open doors in one's career, while a lack of these habits might leave you stagnant and overlooked.

Positive habits, such as regular exercise, healthy eating, disciplined work routines, and continuous learning, contribute to long-term well-being and success. Conversely, negative habits, like neglecting health, indulging in excessive screen time, or avoiding responsibilities, can have detrimental effects on both personal and professional life. Bad habits are like weeds in a garden. At first, they might seem harmless—a small, insignificant growth that's easy to overlook. But if left unchecked, they begin to spread, taking root deep in the soil and entwining themselves with the healthy plants. Over time, they start to choke the life out of the garden, depriving the good plants of the nutrients, sunlight, and space they need to thrive.

Just as a gardener must regularly tend to the garden, pulling out the weeds before they take over, we must be vigilant in our lives, identifying and addressing bad habits before they become too entrenched. The longer we ignore them, the harder they are to remove, and the more damage they cause. But with consistent effort and attention, the garden can be restored to its natural beauty, just as our lives can flourish when we rid ourselves of destructive habits.

If we talk about Spirituality, Spiritual traditions across the world emphasize the profound impact of habits on one's spiritual journey and overall well-being. **The power of habits is often linked to the development of character, the purification of the mind, and the realization of a higher purpose.** Here's a look at spiritual wisdom on the power of habits.

The Law of Karma and Repeated Actions

- **Hinduism:** The concept of Karma teaches that our actions, when repeated, shape our destiny. Good habits (samskaras) lead to positive karma and spiritual growth, while negative habits lead to suffering and spiritual stagnation. The practice of daily rituals (sadhana) and discipline (tapas) is emphasized to cultivate virtuous habits.

- **Quote:** "We are what our thoughts have made us; so take care about what you think. Words are secondary. Thoughts live; they travel far." — Swami Vivekananda

The Power of Virtue and Discipline

- **Christianity:** In Christianity, virtues such as patience, humility, and charity are habits that must be cultivated through regular practice. The teachings of Jesus emphasize the importance of forming habits of love, kindness, and forgiveness. Discipline in prayer, scripture reading, and acts of service is seen as crucial for spiritual growth.

- **Quote:** "Do not be deceived: God cannot be mocked. A man reaps what he sows." — Galatians 6:7

Purification of the Heart

- **Sufism:** In Sufism, the spiritual journey is one of purifying the heart (qalb) from negative habits and tendencies. Regular practices like Dhikr (remembrance of God) and muraqabah (meditation) are encouraged to develop habits of constant awareness of God and inner purification.

- **Quote:** "Your task is not to seek for love, but merely to seek and find all the barriers within yourself that you have built against it." - Rumi

Transformation Through Discipline

- **Judaism:** Jewish teachings emphasize the importance of regular observance of commandments (mitzvot) and study of the Torah. These habits are seen as paths to holiness and righteousness. The practice of daily prayer, reflection, and acts of kindness is integral to spiritual growth and community life.

- **Quote:** "Great is study, for it leads to action." — Talmud, Kiddushin 40b

The Power of Good Deeds

- **Sikhism:** In Sikhism, daily prayer, meditation on God's name (Naam Japna), and performing selfless service (Seva) are emphasized as habitual practices that purify the mind and soul. These habits are believed to bring one closer to God and lead to a life of humility, contentment, and divine grace.

- **Quote:** "He alone is a devotee who practices the teachings. O Nanak, he merges with the Lord, like water with water." — Guru Granth Sahib

What Can You Do to Overcome the Trap?

The Challenge of Breaking Bad Habits

Bad habits are like accumulating junk in a closet. At first, it might seem convenient to just shove things in there, but over time, the clutter builds up. What was once a small mess becomes a major obstacle, making it difficult to find or access what you need. To restore order, you must sort through the clutter, decide what to keep or discard, and reorganize. Similarly, addressing bad habits requires sorting through the negative behaviors, understanding their impact, and making conscious efforts to replace them with positive habits.

Bad habits are often hard to break because they become ingrained in our daily routines. Buddhism teaches that attachment to harmful habits arises from ignorance and craving (tanha).

> *"It is a man's own mind, not his enemy or foe, that lures him to evil ways."*
> — *Buddha*

Bad habits are like a comfortable bed, easy to get into, but hard to get out of.

Overcoming them will require awareness, willpower, and a structured approach to replace them with positive habits. This process can be difficult, but the rewards of living a life guided by healthy, productive habits are immense. Trust me on this. Bad habits generate bad karma and will bind the soul, create suffering, and distance individuals from their true nature or divine essence. *The path to overcoming bad habits involves self-awareness, discipline, prayer, and consistent practice of virtues.* Consistency is the key word here. Success in any area of life often comes down to consistency. Whether it's exercising, practicing a skill, or working toward a goal, the key is to make small, positive actions a regular part of your life. This consistency will eventually lead to significant improvements and achievements.

Build a Habit Loop: Understanding the habit loop – cue, routine, and reward – can help in developing and maintaining positive habits

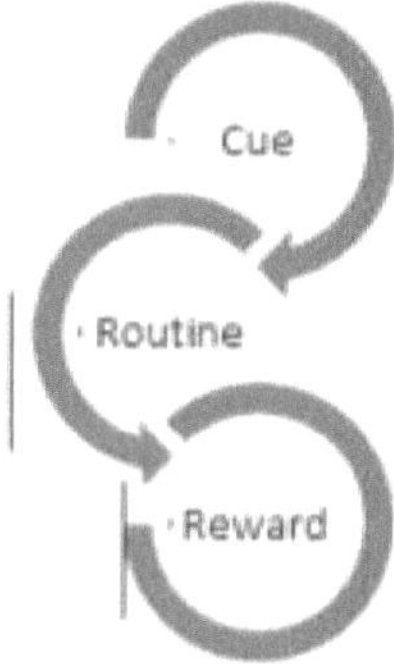

1. Identify the Cue

The Cue is the trigger that will initiate the habit. It could be a specific time of day, an emotional state, a particular location, or a preceding action. The cue will signal your brain to start the habit, so identifying and being consistent with it is crucial.

Examples of Cues:

- **Time:** Brushing your teeth every morning when you wake up.

- **Location:** Drinking a glass of water as soon as you enter the kitchen.

- **Emotional State:** Going for a walk when you feel stressed.

Establish the Routine

The Routine is the behavior that you want to turn into a habit. It's the action that follows the cue. This is the part of the loop that will require the most effort from you, especially in the beginning, until it becomes automatic.

Examples of Routines:

- **Physical:** Going for a jog after waking up.

- **Mental:** Meditating for 10 minutes when you feel anxious.

- **Behavioral:** Reading a book instead of scrolling through social media before bed.

Create the Reward

The Reward is the benefit you get from completing the routine. Reinforce positive habits by rewarding yourself when you achieve milestones. This can create a positive association with the habit, making it more likely to stick. It reinforces the habit loop, making your brain more likely to repeat the routine in the future. Rewards can be intrinsic (feeling good, a sense of accomplishment) or extrinsic (tangible rewards like a treat or a break).

Examples of Rewards:

- **Physical:** A relaxing shower after a workout.

- **Emotional:** A sense of calm after meditating.

- **Tangible:** Allowing yourself a small treat after completing a task.

Pearls of Wisdom

The Practice of Yoga and Meditation

The Gita advocates for the practice of yoga and meditation as a means to control the mind and overcome bad habits.

- **Verse:** "By restraining his senses and fixing his consciousness upon Me, the yogi who is of a disciplined mind is said to have attained spiritual union." (Bhagavad Gita 6:18)

- **Interpretation:** Regular practice of yoga and meditation helps in gaining control over the mind and senses, making it easier to break free from bad habits. This spiritual discipline leads to inner peace and the cultivation of positive, life-affirming habits.

Putting on the New Self

The Bible teaches that through faith in Christ, believers are called to put off their old selves, which are characterized by sinful behaviors and bad habits, and to put on a new self that reflects the character of Christ.

- **Verse:** "You were taught, with regard to your former way of life, to put off your old self, which is being corrupted by its deceitful desires; to be made new in the attitude of your minds; and to put on the new self, created to be like God in true righteousness and holiness." (Ephesians 4:22-24)

- **Interpretation:** This passage emphasizes the need for a complete transformation, where believers let go of their old habits and behaviors and embrace a new way of living that aligns with God's righteousness and holiness.

Ignoring the power of habits is a common trap that can lead to a lack of direction and achievement in life. By recognizing the importance of habits and actively working to develop positive ones, you can create a foundation for lasting success and fulfillment. By cultivating positive habits rooted in mindfulness, discipline, and consistent practice, individuals can align their lives with higher principles, leading to a more meaningful and spiritually fulfilling existence.

The Trap of Underestimating the Value of Patience

The Haste Trap

Rainer Maria Rilke, in his "Letters to a Young Poet," encourages patience during periods of waiting: "**Be patient toward all that is unsolved in your heart**." Silence cultivates this patience, helping us endure while we await clarity and resolution.

In a world increasingly defined by instant gratification, rapid technological advancements, and the relentless pursuit of efficiency, the virtue of patience has found itself relegated to the sidelines. In today's world, where speed, efficiency, and instant results are prized, the idea of "waiting" often seems contrary to prevailing values. Patience has taken a backseat to the rush for immediate gratification and constant productivity.. However, I feel underestimating the value of patience is not just a philosophical misstep; it is a profound loss of wisdom that has been cherished across cultures, religions, and philosophies for millennia.

Patience is often misunderstood as passive waiting or inaction. On the contrary, patience is an active state of perseverance and restraint, a conscious choice to endure without succumbing to impulsive behavior. In psychological terms, patience is a higher-order cognitive function that involves self-regulation, delayed gratification, and a lot of emotional intelligence. It is what differentiates a mature, rational human being from a child who wants immediate satisfaction. *The famous Stanford marshmallow experiment, for example, revealed that children who exhibited patience by waiting for a larger reward tended to have better life outcomes compared to those who opted for immediate but smaller rewards.* This speaks volumes about the role of patience in cultivating discipline, focus, and resilience—qualities essential for personal growth.

For the Stoics, patience was linked to the concept of **"Amor Fati"**—the love of one's fate. Thereby, patience is the acceptance of life's unfolding with equanimity, not as a resignation but as an active embrace of reality, however it may present itself. *This acceptance does not mean passivity but rather a recognition that some things are beyond our control, and to rage against them is to waste one's energy on fruitless endeavors.*

In The Bhagavad Gita, a sacred Hindu text, it is advised to maintain steadiness of mind amidst the dualities of success and failure, pleasure and pain, gain and loss. But what helps to maintain such steadiness? Well, the answer is patience.

The increasing prevalence of anxiety, stress, and burnout in modern society can be partly attributed to one's inability to wait, reflect, and process. **When speed becomes the ultimate value, depth is lost.** Relationships suffer, as patience is key to understanding, empathy, and compromise. Patience can only enable you to support others emotionally. It will give room for understanding one another's feelings, needs, and insecurities, fostering a sense of safety and trust. When you are in a relationship, you both are on your own journey of personal growth. Patience allows each person to grow at their own pace and in their own way, which, in turn, strengthens the relationship. *In relationships, impatience manifests as a lack of understanding, empathy, and willingness to listen.* When we are impatient, we may push others to meet our expectations, jump to conclusions, or become easily frustrated with their pace. This behavior can damage relationships by creating unnecessary tension, misunderstandings, and conflicts. Healthy relationships require patience to understand each other's perspectives, work through differences, and grow together.

The Chinese bamboo tree is famous for its growth pattern. **After the seed is planted, the tree doesn't break through the ground for five years.** During all this time, it requires constant watering, fertilizing, and care. **But in the fifth year, it suddenly grows up to 90 feet in just six weeks!** This analogy illustrates that patience involves nurturing and caring for something even when there are no visible results. It shows that progress often happens beneath the surface and that perseverance and patience are required for a dramatic breakthrough. So, reclaiming patience involves conscious effort—mindfulness practices, intentional slow living, and cultivating environments (both personal and professional) that value depth over speed. It is about creating a culture that recognizes the importance of thoughtful decision-making, meaningful relationships, and genuine human connections.

Wanting immediate results or success can lead to frustration and poor decisions. Whether in choosing a career path, making an investment, or entering a relationship, acting too quickly can lead to poor choices that may have long-term repercussions. Many people find themselves regretting decisions made in moments of impatience, realizing only later that a more thoughtful and deliberate approach would have yielded better results. *Patience is not merely about waiting; it is about maintaining a calm and steady mindset in the face of delays, challenges, or adversity.* When we underestimate patience, we overlook its ability to give us inner strength. Patience allows us to stay focused and composed, preventing rash decisions that could lead to regret. Patience is like weaving a tapestry. Each thread you add contributes to the overall pattern, but it takes time to see the complete picture. If you rush the process or become frustrated, the threads might become tangled, and the pattern could be disrupted. Patience helps you carefully and deliberately create a beautiful and intricate design, ensuring that each step contributes to the final, harmonious result.

On a deeper level, impatience can prevent one from achieving inner peace and spiritual growth. **Most spiritual traditions teach the value of patience as a means to connect more deeply with oneself and the Universe.** Impatience, on the other hand, keeps the mind restless, always seeking the next moment rather than being present in the now. It obstructs practices like meditation, mindfulness, and contemplation, which require stillness and patience to truly benefit from.

Regret over impatience is a common, yet deeply felt experience. It is a trap. Many people look back on their lives and realize that impatience led them to make hasty decisions, miss valuable opportunities, or create unnecessary conflict. This trap often carries a sense of lost potential—a recognition that if only they had waited, shown more restraint, or taken the time to understand, their path might have been different and perhaps more fulfilling. Turn the **trap of impatience** into a valuable **example before it's too late.**

You can create a personal mantra that reflects your commitment to patience. It could be something like, **"Good things take time,"** or **"Trust the process."** Repeat this mantra whenever you feel the urge to rush or become impatient. This mantra becomes a powerful anchor that reminds you of the importance of taking your time and acting thoughtfully.

Create Reminders of Patience's Value

Develop reminders or practices that reinforce the value of patience in your daily life. These could be visual cues, like quotes or affirmations placed around your living or working space, or mental exercises like mindfulness meditation that help cultivate patience. When faced with a choice that requires patience, recalling past mistakes can help you pause and consider a more measured approach.

Here's how you can turn the trap of impatience into an example:

1. **Identify Specific Instances of Impatience**

    Reflect on specific moments in life where impatience led to mistakes or regrets. For example, you might recall a time when you made a hasty decision to change jobs without fully considering the implications, only to realize later that the new job was not a good fit. Identifying these instances helps bring clarity to the pattern of impatience and its consequences.

2. **Acknowledge the Consequences**

    Understand the impact that impatience had in those situations. Did it lead to financial loss, damaged relationships, missed opportunities, or personal dissatisfaction? Acknowledging the consequences is crucial for understanding why impatience is a trap – it blinds us to potential risks and rewards and often leaves us worse off.

3. **Extract the Lessons Learned**

    Instead of dwelling on regret, focus on what each experience taught you. For instance, a rushed decision to invest in a business without proper research may have resulted in a loss. However, it also taught you the importance of due diligence, patience in planning, and making informed choices. These lessons are valuable not just for yourself but can also be shared as advice to others.

4. **Reframe the Narrative**

    Change how you view your moments of impatience. Instead of seeing them purely as mistakes, see them as necessary steps in your growth journey. **Everyone has moments where they act too quickly or rashly; what matters is how those moments shape your future behavior.** By reframing impatience as a teacher rather than a failure, you empower yourself to move forward with greater wisdom.

5. **Apply the Lessons Proactively**

    Use the insights gained from past impatience to make more deliberate and thoughtful decisions in the present and future. For instance, if you've learned that rushing into relationships or commitments leads to disappointment, you might decide to take more time to get to know someone or fully evaluate a situation before committing. This proactive approach turns your past impatience into a guiding example.

Using Impatience as a Tool for Growth

By turning the trap of impatience into an example, you transform a negative pattern into a source of wisdom. You learn to embrace patience not only as a virtue but as a practical strategy for making better decisions, building stronger relationships, and leading a more fulfilling life. When viewed through this lens, impatience is no longer a trap but a stepping stone toward greater understanding and personal evolution.

The Spiritual Dimension: Patience as a Path to Enlightenment

Patience + Silence = Peace

Magic of Patience

On a deeper, spiritual level, patience is more than a virtue; it is a path to self-realization. Patience is the force that allows an individual to keep moving forward despite setbacks, transforming every challenge into an opportunity for growth.

Spiritual masters from various traditions have emphasized that patience is a necessary foundation for meditation, prayer, and self-inquiry. It allows the mind to settle, to move beyond superficial thoughts and emotions, and to access deeper states of consciousness. Patience cultivates humility, for it teaches us that not everything will unfold according to our desires or timelines.

From **Shandilya Upanishad's** 1ˢᵗ Chapter:

Under Niyama (religious observances) are ten, namely, Tapas, Santosha, Astikya, Dana, Ishvarapujana, Siddhanta-Sravana, Hrih, Mati, Japa, and Vrata.

Of these Tapas, the emancipation of the body is achieved through the observances of such penances as Krichchhra, Chandrayana, (both are types of fasts), **etc** which purify the body and mind. Tapas helps in cultivating self-control and endurance, leading to spiritual growth and inner strength. Santosha is being satisfied with whatever comes to us of its own accord.

In the Rigveda, one of the oldest and most sacred scriptures of Hinduism, patience is praised as a divine quality that leads to prosperity and happiness.

BG 16.3

तेजः क्षमा धृतिः शौचमद्रोहो नातिमानिता। भवन्ति सम्पदं दैवीमभिजातस्य
भारत।।16.3।।
tejaḥ kṣhamā dhṛitiḥ śhaucham adroho nāti-mānitā bhavanti sampadaṁ
daivīm abhijātasya bhārata

Translation: (TejH) brilliance, (kshma) forgiveness, (dhrtiH) patience, (shaucham) purity, (adrohH) absence of hostility, (naatimaanita) not seeking honor for oneself, (bharat) O Arjun! (daiveem, sampadam) devotional nature, (abhijaatasya) characteristics of a person born with, person born with devotional nature are.

Translation: Brilliance, forgiveness, patience, purity, absence of hostility, do not seek honor for oneself, O Arjun! These are the characteristics of a person born with a devotional nature.

Patience involves the capacity to endure difficulties and delays without frustration. It represents a calm and steady mindset in the face of challenges.

As per the Rig Veda, "Patience is the highest virtue, patience is the highest tapas (austerity), patience is the highest dharma, patience is the highest brahman (supreme reality)."

Magic of Silence

Silence is a profound ally during periods of waiting, as echoed by the wisdom of great thinkers and sages throughout history. By embracing silence, we transform our waiting into opportunities for reflection, growth, and clarity, ultimately enhancing our resilience and capacity to navigate life's challenges. In the words of **Khalil Gibran**, "Your soul is oftentimes a battlefield, but in silence, it finds its peace."

The importance of silence in the context of the Upanishads, along with insights from sages and relevant quotes, emphasizes its transformative power, especially in coping with difficulties and challenges. Here's how silence can help during such times:

1. Inner Strength and Resilience

Silence fosters inner strength, allowing individuals to gather their thoughts and emotions. As the sage Patanjali said, "In the stillness of the mind, one finds strength." This resilience can help one face obstacles with a calm and composed demeanor.

2. Clarity and Insight

The Upanishads teach that silence is a state where true knowledge can emerge. In the Brihadaranyaka Upanishad, it is stated, "In silence, the highest truth can be known." This clarity helps in making informed decisions during challenging times.

3. Acceptance of the Present Moment

Silence encourages acceptance of the current situation. The Katha Upanishad highlights the importance of understanding the impermanent nature of life. Embracing silence allows one to accept difficulties as part of the journey, fostering patience.

4. Connection with the Divine

Silence is seen as a way to connect with the divine or universal consciousness. **The Taittiriya Upanishad teaches that, in silence, one can experience the essence of bliss (Ananda), which helps individuals find solace and hope during tough times.**

5. Emotional Regulation

Sages often emphasized the role of silence in managing emotions. As the wise words of Lao Tzu suggest, "Silence is a source of great strength." By practicing silence, one can regulate emotions and respond to challenges more thoughtfully rather than reactively.

6. Cultivating Patience

The act of being silent can cultivate patience. **As the Chandogya Upanishad illustrates, waiting and reflecting in silence can lead to greater understanding and wisdom.** This patience allows one to navigate obstacles without rushing into decisions.

7. Meditative Practice

Engaging in silent meditation can provide a refuge during difficult times. As the sage Ramana Maharshi said, "The stillness of the mind leads to liberation." This practice can be grounding and help one cope with stress and uncertainty.

Quotes to Reflect On

- "Silence is the true friend that never betrays." - Confucius.
- "In silence, we can hear the whispers of our soul." - Unknown

Discovering Opportunities and Lessons in Silence

1. Enhancing Awareness and Mindfulness: Observe the Hidden

Silence cultivates a heightened sense of awareness, allowing us to engage fully with the present moment. By approaching this stillness with openness, curiosity, and acceptance, we can observe the nuances, patterns, and interconnections that often go unnoticed.

2. Fostering Gratitude and Appreciation: Cultivate the Joy

In the quiet of silence, we can deepen our sense of gratitude. By recognizing the inherent value, beauty, and goodness in our lives—be it our relationships, our circumstances, or our personal qualities—we cultivate joy and express appreciation for the richness that surrounds us.

3. Promoting Growth and Understanding: Reframe perspectives

Silence provides a fertile ground for reflection, enabling us to examine our experiences, thoughts, and emotions. This introspection can lead to profound insights, expanding our perspectives and enhancing our knowledge and skills as we navigate life's lessons.

By embracing silence, we not only find clarity, but also unlock a wealth of opportunities for growth, gratitude, and understanding during our waiting periods.

Preparing for Outcomes Through Silence

Silence can really help you in tough times or when you are facing obstacles.

1. Building Confidence and Resilience

Silence can be a powerful ally in boosting our confidence. When we take time to sit quietly with our thoughts, we start to trust ourselves more. For example, think about a time you faced a tough decision. In that quiet space, you might have realized that you have the skills to handle whatever comes your way. Facing those fears—whether it's public speaking or a challenging work project—becomes easier when we take a moment to breathe and reflect.

2. Cultivating Acceptance and Surrender

Waiting often comes with expectations, and those can create stress. Silence helps us let go of those pressures. Picture a situation where you're waiting for news—like a job application or a medical test result. In that stillness, you can practice acceptance. Instead of clinging to what you hope will happen, you can embrace the uncertainty. **This doesn't mean you stop caring; rather, you open yourself to whatever outcome may come, which can bring a sense of peace.**

3. Aligning with Your Higher Purpose

Silence is a wonderful way to connect with your deeper self. **It's like tuning into a radio station that plays the music of your true nature.** When you take time to be silent—maybe through meditation or just a quiet walk—you can reflect on what truly matters to you. For instance, if you're trying to figure out your next steps in life, this inner dialogue can help you understand your passions and align with your goals. It's about listening to that little voice that guides you toward your purpose.

By embracing silence, we not only prepare for the outcomes of our waiting but also cultivate a greater sense of clarity and alignment with our life's journey. Whether it's facing challenges with newfound confidence, accepting life's uncertainties, or connecting with your higher purpose, silence can be a transformative experience.

How to Embrace Silence?

One of the most effective ways to embrace silence during periods of waiting is through meditation. This practice involves focusing our attention on a single object—whether it's our breath, a mantra, a sound, or a visual image—and observing our thoughts, feelings, and sensations without judgment. Meditation not only calms the mind and relaxes the body but also enhances our overall well-being.

Benefits of Meditation

Through meditation, we can cultivate awareness, improve concentration, and gain deeper insights. It opens the door to higher states of consciousness, such as bliss, peace, or even enlightenment. For instance, **Thich Nhat Hanh**, a renowned Zen master, emphasized that meditation helps us be present and fully experience each moment, allowing us to navigate life's challenges with grace.

Meditating on Symbols of Strength: Learn from Lord Shiva

While you can meditate on any object that resonates with you, one particularly powerful image is that of **Shiva seated on a tiger skin**. This symbol represents not only strength and power but also patience and mastery over our instincts. By visualizing this image, we can tap into the profound wisdom of patience and align ourselves with the cosmic order. In the *Shiva Purana*, we see Shiva as both a fierce destroyer and a compassionate creator. His ability to destroy the old to make way for the new is not impulsive; it is deliberate and rooted in a deep understanding of cosmic timing. Similarly, when we meditate on Shiva, we are reminded of the importance of **patience** and **calm contemplation** before taking action.

In life, many of us rush into decisions, often driven by fear, anxiety, or a sense of urgency. But Shiva teaches us that **wise action arises from stillness**. Just as he contemplates for long periods before making decisions that affect the entire universe, we too can cultivate the wisdom to wait and reflect, trusting that the right moment will present itself when the conditions are aligned.

WHO

GUIDING YOU TO DISCOVER YOUR TRUE SELF AND
UNDERSTAND YOUR CONNECTION TO THE WORLD.

WHO

Q.1 Who is a superior person?

Ans: A superior person might be someone who demonstrates strong moral values, shows kindness and empathy, and acts with integrity. They often inspire others, communicate effectively, and have a growth mindset, continually striving to improve themselves and help those around them. It's also about the impact they have on their community and the positive changes they foster. Here's a breakdown of the qualities of a superior person, along with analogies to illustrate each one more vividly:

1. **Authenticity**

    Like a well-crafted mirror, an authentic person reflects their true self without distortion. Just as a mirror shows what is truly there, they embody their values and beliefs openly, inviting others to see them as they are. Consider someone who stands up for their beliefs in a discussion, even when it's unpopular. They speak their truth, knowing that authenticity fosters trust.

2. **Empathy**

    Empathy is like a bridge connecting two islands. It allows one person to cross over to another's experiences and feelings, creating understanding and support. Imagine a friend comforting someone who has lost a loved one. They listen deeply, sharing in the pain rather than offering empty platitudes, making the other person feel seen and supported.

3. Integrity

Integrity is like a sturdy tree with deep roots. It stands tall through storms, unwavering in its principles, providing shade and shelter to those in need. A business leader who refuses to engage in unethical practices, even when it would be easy to cut corners for profit, exemplifies integrity. They prioritize honesty, earning the respect of their team. In a romantic relationship, one partner feels overwhelmed with work and communicates this to their significant other rather than withdrawing emotionally. This transparency helps both partners navigate the situation together, fostering deeper understanding and support.

4. Wisdom

Wisdom is like a compass that guides travelers. It helps navigate through life's complexities, pointing toward what is right and beneficial. An experienced mentor who shares lessons learned from their own failures and successes helps others make informed choices, embodying the essence of wisdom.

5. Resilience

Resilience is like a rubber band that stretches but doesn't break. It can adapt to pressure and return to its original shape, ready to face challenges anew. An athlete who trains hard after an injury, using the setback as motivation to improve, demonstrates resilience. They maintain focus on their goals despite difficulties.

6. Service Orientation

Service orientation is like a lighthouse guiding ships safely to shore. It shines a light on the needs of others, helping to navigate toward safety and support. A volunteer who dedicates time to helping the homeless demonstrates a service-oriented mindset, always looking for ways to uplift others in their community.

7. Open-Mindedness

Open-mindedness is like a garden that welcomes diverse plants. Each new flower adds beauty and richness, contributing to a vibrant ecosystem. An **open-minded person** is willing to acknowledge and explore different ideas, cultures, perspectives, and concepts. A team member who actively seeks out and values different perspectives during discussions fosters creativity and innovation, demonstrating open-mindedness.

You want to Discern a Superior Person

1. **Observe Actions**: Look for consistency between their words and actions. Superior individuals often demonstrate integrity and authenticity in various situations.

2. **Listen to Their Words**: Pay attention to how they communicate: do they speak with kindness, understanding, and respect? Do they encourage others?

3. **Notice Their Relationships**: Superior people tend to build strong, meaningful connections with others. Observe how they interact with friends, family, and strangers.

4. **Evaluate Their Response to Challenges**: Watch how they handle adversity. A superior person usually exhibits resilience and grace under pressure.

5. **Seek Their Advice**: Ask for their insights on challenges or decisions. Their wisdom and perspective can often illuminate their character.

A person who is ever evolving holistically and spiritually is a superior person. Let's delve deeper into each sense and how they contribute to the journey of becoming a superior person.

1. Eyes: Vision Beyond the Visible

- **Spiritual Insight:** The ability to see beyond the physical realm allows for a deeper understanding of life's complexities. A person with spiritual vision discerns underlying truths and meanings in experiences and relationships, fostering wisdom and empathy.

- o **Intuition**: This sense encourages trusting one's intuition and inner guidance, allowing one to navigate life with greater clarity and purpose.

2. **Nose: Discernment**

   - o **Moral and Ethical Awareness**: Just as the nose distinguishes between scents, a superior person develops a keen sense of discernment to differentiate between good and evil, truth and falsehood. This discernment is crucial in decision-making and relationships, enabling them to uphold integrity and authenticity.

   - o **Intuition about Environments**: They can also sense the emotional and spiritual climates of situations, allowing for more compassionate interactions.

3. **Tongue: Spiritual Taste**

   - o **Desire for Knowledge**: The tongue represents a craving for deeper understanding and wisdom. A superior person continuously seeks knowledge, fostering a lifelong commitment to learning and growth.

   - o **Expression of Truth**: Additionally, this sense reflects the importance of communication. Speaking truthfully and kindly enhances relationships and builds community, echoing the idea that words have power.

4. **Ears: Faith Through Hearing**

   - o **Active Listening**: This sense emphasizes the importance of listening, not just to words but to the deeper meanings and emotions behind them. A superior person cultivates the ability to hear others, fostering connections and understanding.

   - o **Receptivity to Wisdom**: By engaging with spiritual texts and teachings, individuals open themselves to insights that can transform their lives and beliefs.

5. **Skin: Touch and Connection**

    o   **Empathy and Compassion:** The sense of touch symbolizes the ability to connect with others on a deeper level. Whether through physical touch or emotional support, this sense enhances relationships and facilitates healing.

    o   **Transference of Energy:** In spiritual practices, the act of laying on hands symbolizes the transfer of divine energy, reflecting the interconnectedness of all beings. A superior person recognizes the power of their presence and actions in the lives of others.

Conclusion

By cultivating awareness and mastery of these senses, a person evolves into a superior being, one who not only seeks personal growth but also contributes positively to the world around them. This journey involves continuous reflection, learning, and connection, ultimately leading to a more profound understanding of life and a deeper sense of purpose.

Q.2 Who is a truly happy person?

Ans: One with deep equanimity from within is a happy person. Inward happiness has everything to do with your soul. Your soul is the root of your being. **A man who is buried under the heap of hatred, jealousy, tension, anxiety, worry, and many other negative states of mind can never be a happy person.** To be truly happy, you have to unburden your soul from all these vices. Remove these, and you will start uncovering the seeds of happiness gradually. It is happiness that is eternal and liberating. Without the purification of mind and soul, a person can't find true happiness. A blow of the above is just enough to fan the flames of unhappiness. Only the purification of the soul and its nourishment can make the roots of happiness grow stronger. This is an eternal truth, and only the realization of this and knowledge of truth we experience, not the ignorance of it, that makes us joyful and happy. **As happiness enters the mind through the front door, restlessness and excitement leave the mind through the back door.**

Difference between Excitement and Happiness

The excited person's behavior is quite different from that of a happy person. When someone, for instance, is excited, he or she expresses his or her excitement by smiling, laughing, whistling, singing, dancing, kissing, hugging, running, crying or even saying things which he or she would never otherwise say under any circumstance. *When real happiness arises, however, the person does not express anything either verbally or physically but remains calm, peaceful, composed, and serene, for it is this real happiness that leads his mind to true concentration.* As we know, it is not excitement but just the opposite of it that leads the mind to concentration. As the concentrated mind generates sufficient quietness of the mind, instead of expressing any mental agitation, a truly happy person sees the truth as it is. The real knowledge of the truth makes a person wise enough to be happy in the deepest sense of the word.

ENLIGHTENING WISDOM: Your spiritual guide

As per Guru Granth Sahib, causes of dukh are taunts (*fika-bol*) (15-14), hypocrisy (*pakhand*) (28-17), and loss of wealth (*dhan*) (p. 59-14). Drinking of wine results in madness (*baral*) (554-14) that is characterized by sadness, hopelessness (*niraasa*), pollution of the intellect, restlessness, and misery, and can lead to all sorts of diseases (*rog*) (p. 279 and 280). The text also mentions three factors that are bad for the body and mental peace (24-16; 19-11) and can cause depression: excessive and unfulfilled sexual desire (*kaam*), anger (*krodha*), and egotism or pride (*ahankaar*) (p. 51). These have been variously referred to as demons (*paret*) (513-13) and wounds of the soul (*jeeah mei chot*) (152-11). The text also sums up by pointing toward a desire and love for materialistic things (*love of maya*) as the root cause of all diseases leading to *dukh*. It is said that one may not feel interested in his or her work like acting in dramas or singing in theaters, or riding horses or elephants. There is also a loss of interest in grooming oneself with jewelry and dressing in silk and satin clothes (p. 225), representing self-neglect. Bad *karmic* actions force a person to sit and weep (15-11).

The text also mentions that the afflicted mind (*muhn-bhulo*) may harbor negative thoughts (*vikar*) (222-3). The sick person perceives everyone else as sick, while to the happy person, everyone else seems happy, and also that for the depressed, colors may appear faded and washed away (27-19). Weeping (*rona*) (316-16) and loss of sleep (*neend*) and appetite have been mentioned as symptoms of sadness seen after the person is separated from the Lord (244-19), as is heaviness on the head (*sir aavey bhaar*) (222-3). The tongue is said to lose all tastes in the absence of the name of the Lord (354-16); all tastes (saad) are perceived as insipid and bland (*fika*) (218-15; 385-4). **In the absence of the Lord, one becomes *dukhi*, so it can be interpreted that loss of taste is mentioned as a symptom of *dukh*.** The afflicted person may also have poor self-care and may be dressed in filthy cloths (*mailey veis*). A reference to hopelessness as a symptom probably is reflected in the following line: *In front of me, I see the jungle burning; behind me, I see green plants sprouting* (20-4).

It also suggests meditation as having a therapeutic effect, provided it is done with the Lord's name in mind. Through meditation and listening to religious scholars and spiritual teachers, devotees are forever in bliss.

The text enumerates many ways of praying (*pujaa, bhagti*) to the Lord, some of which include: *Ardaas* (prayer), *shabadand kirtan* (holy songs), *naam-jaap* (chanting the Name), *oostuht* (praising the Lord), listening to *saakhi* (Guru's teachings), *gurbani* (Guru's words), and *upadeis* (teachings). It notes that grief gets resolved by coming to the sanctuary of the *parbrahma* (sanctuary here may refer to any holy place) (132-19).

For a more long-term control and management of sadness, the text recommends remembering (*simran*) and praising the Lord (p. 1421) and staying in His sanctuary (*raam ki saran*). Only these will lead to eternal peace (p. 1427) and balance within the mind (674-10). Chanting the name of the Lord (*har-jap*) and dedicating oneself to selfless service (*sevaa*) of others (110-1) enable the individual to attain happiness (21-10). **The name can be chanted 24 hours a day (*aath pahar*) (901-7) or day and night (896-18), and this serves as a protective and therapeutic measure for *dukh* (23-5).** Thus, the *agurmukhi* way of life has been recommended (21-10).

Without the Guru, one loses their way and wanders around in the forest (57-3). The Guru has been equated to the Lord (442-18) who resolves our affairs (*kaaj sawaarey*) (13-15) and to a ladder, a boat, and a raft carrying the victim across the "*world-ocean*," which is probably the metaphor for melancholy. He is known to fulfill the hopes of the hopeless (p17), revealing the path to peace (60-9) and having the quality of empathy (*soorat*) (intuitive understanding; page 18-3). When one involves themselves in the service of the Guru, peace (61-5) and intuitive balance (*sahaj*; p. 68-5) are obtained.

Through the Guru's sermons,pain and pleasure become alike (131-12), and joy (*harakh*) and sorrow (*sog*) feel the same to one's consciousness (214-13). The Guru's word has been equated with *amrat* (ambrosia) (185-5); suffering (*dukh*), agony (*klesh*), and fear (*bhau*) do not cling to those whose heart is filled with the *Gurumantra* (51-4). The mind, body, and soul, all are appeased (47-19). Those who suffer keep on wandering around the world begging but get exhausted and find a solution only with the *Guru* in his teachings (p. 34). The solution is usually a *jaap* (chant), by which the name of the Lord and hence peace comes to dwell in the mind of the diseased (p. 34), leading to the state of *moksha/mokha* (salvation) (114-11). The *Guru's* word saves one from falling into hell (177-8), which may again refer to melancholy.

Hinduism

Sat Chit Ananda is a Sanskrit word that refers to the nature of authenticity as it is abstracted in yogic philosophy and Hindu philosophy. Some contemplate *Sat Chit Ananda* to be the same as Brahman or God (Absolute Genuineness).

Sat Chit Ananda is a Sanskrit word that refers to the nature of authenticity as it is abstracted in yogic philosophy and Hindu philosophy. Some contemplate Sat Chit Ananda to be the same as Brahman or God (Absolute Genuineness). Sat – to be here and now, Chit - to be totally aware at every moment, to be conscious - Ananda – To be in a total blissful state, to be eternally joyful. Sat Chit Ananda represents a holistic understanding of existence, consciousness, and bliss. By embodying these principles, individuals can move toward a state of greater authenticity and fulfillment. This perspective invites us to explore our inner landscape, fostering peace and joy in our lives. Happiness or freedom from suffering arises in a silent mind that is free from modifications (vrittis) and duality.

The concept of **Sat Chit Ananda** is a profound expression of the nature of reality and consciousness in yogic and Hindu philosophy. Here's a deeper exploration of its components and implications:

Components of Sat Chit Ananda

1. **Sat (Being)**

   o **Meaning**: This refers to existence or reality. It emphasizes the importance of being present in the here and now, grounding oneself in the present moment. This state of being is often contrasted with the distractions of the past or future, encouraging us to experience life fully as it unfolds.

2. **Chit (Consciousness)**

   o **Meaning**: Chit signifies awareness and consciousness. It represents the ability to be fully aware of one's thoughts, feelings, and surroundings. This heightened awareness allows for deeper understanding and connection with oneself and the Universe, fostering clarity and insight.

3. **Ananda (Bliss)**

   o **Meaning**: Ananda denotes a state of eternal bliss and joy. It is a deeper, lasting happiness that transcends temporary pleasures. This bliss arises from a profound connection to one's true nature and the realization of unity with all existence.

Philosophical Implications

- **Unity with Brahman**: Sat Chit Ananda is often equated with Brahman, the ultimate reality or the divine source in Hindu philosophy. Realizing this state means recognizing that our true nature is not separate from the cosmos but part of an infinite whole.

- **Freedom from Suffering**: True happiness and freedom from suffering come from a mind that is silent and free from distractions and modifications (vrittis). When the mind is calm and undisturbed, one can experience the inherent joy and peace of existence.

- **Overcoming Duality**: The state of Sat Chit Ananda transcends dualistic thinking (such as good vs. bad, pleasure vs. pain). This duality often leads to conflict and suffering. By embracing the oneness of all things, one can find peace and harmony within.

ये हि संस्पर्शजा भोगा दु:खयोनय एव ते |

आद्यन्तवन्त: कौन्तेय न तेषु रमते बुध: || 22||

ye hi sansparsha-jā bhogā duḥkha-yonaya eva te

ādyantavantaḥ kaunteya na teṣhu ramate budhaḥ

Chapter 5, Verse 22

The pleasure from material objects keeps decreasing as we enjoy it. In Economics, this is defined as the Law of Diminishing Returns. *But the bliss of God is sentient; it is sat-chit-ānand (eternal ever-fresh divine bliss). Hence, one can go on chanting the same divine Name of God all day long and relish ever-new devotional satisfaction in it.*

No sane person enjoying a delicious dessert would be willing to give it up and eat mud instead. Similarly, when one begins to enjoy divine bliss, the mind loses all taste for material pleasures. Those endowed with the faculty of discrimination understand the above three drawbacks of material pleasures and restrain their senses from them.

Dhammapada, verse 201

"To live without anger among the angry is, indeed, happy. To live unafflicted among the afflicted is happy. To live without ambition among the ambitious is happy. To live without possession is a happy life like that of the radiant gods. To live without competition among those who compete is happy, for 'he who wins creates an enemy; and unhappy does the defeated sleep.' The one who is neither a victor nor the defeated sleeps happily."

Key Themes

1. **Living Without Anger**:

   - **Meaning**: Finding happiness in remaining calm amidst chaos. This reflects emotional resilience and the ability to maintain peace even when surrounded by negativity.

2. **Unafflicted Among the Afflicted**:

   - **Meaning**: Experiencing joy while navigating a world full of suffering. It suggests compassion and understanding rather than being dragged down by the pain of others.

3. **Ambition vs. Contentment**:

   - **Meaning**: Happiness can be found in simplicity, free from the relentless pursuit of status or success. It highlights the value of contentment over the constant drive to achieve.

4. **Non-Possession**:

   - **Meaning**: A life free from material attachment leads to greater joy. This concept echoes the idea that true happiness doesn't come from accumulating possessions but from inner fulfillment.

5. **Avoiding Competition**:

   - **Meaning**: Competition can breed resentment and discord. The passage suggests that living without rivalry allows for peaceful coexistence and avoids the pain of victory and defeat. Compete with yourself.

6. **Neutrality and Balance**:

   - **Meaning**: The idea of neither being a victor nor the defeated indicates a balanced approach to life, where one is not defined by external outcomes but finds peace in neutrality.

Q.3 Who should we associate with?

Associating with positive people is like opening windows in a stuffy room; it brings in fresh air and new perspectives.

All the dukkha comes to one not from the wise, but from the foolishness or foolish people. Therefore, we should not associate with a man with little morality, little concentration, and little wisdom, "for the same reason that we most carefully avoid an enraged elephant, a mettlesome horse, a mad bull, or keep away from snakes…"Just as a man of intelligence avoids all these things, so also does he avoid those men who are not fit to associate with and thus he escapes those destructive influences pulling him down in life.

The people we surround ourselves with can significantly impact our mental and emotional state.

According to the *Guru Granth Sahib*, the company that we keep has a marked influence on us, resulting in disastrous consequences if we are not careful.

Jo jaisee sangat milai, so taiso fal khaa-ay. ||86||

According to the company it keeps, so are the fruits it eats. ||86||

"I have been ruined and destroyed by bad company"(SGGS p. 1369). Bhagat Kabir tells us frankly how his life was destroyed due to the companionship of bad sangat.

And it was only by changing this company that salvation and peace were obtained. The **Sri Guru Granth Sahib** emphasizes the profound impact of our friendships and associations on our actions, outlook, and spiritual development. It highlights the importance of engaging with the **sangat** (holy company) of wise and virtuous individuals, which fosters positive qualities such as compassion and integrity. Conversely, the scripture warns against negative influences that can lead one astray. By choosing to surround ourselves with uplifting companions, we not only enhance our personal growth but also support collective spiritual progress, transforming our perspectives and deepening our connection to the divine. Ultimately, the teachings remind us that our associations significantly shape our journey through life.

The Guru says: "False is friendship with the false and greedy. False is its foundation" *(SGGS p 1412)*. The message again is clear; friendship with a fool, an untruthful person, a corrupt being, a *Manmukh* (self-centered, self-willed, a person in worldly consciousness, etc.), a person who is wicked, pompous (proud or arrogant), unrighteous, greedy, unfaithful and so on, is founded on a false foundation; therefore, it will last "for only a few short days" and will "never work out right". Such friendships will lead a person who wishes to embrace the path of righteousness to ruin. (*Dharm*)

BUDDHISM

Verse 328. DHAMMAPADA

Cherish the Company of the Good

If, for practice, one finds a friend

prudent, well-behaved, and wise

Mindful, joyful, live with him.

all troubles overcome.

Explanation: If you come upon a mature, wise companion whose ways are virtuous, you must associate with him so you can lead a happy and alert life, overcoming all dangers.

VERSE 329

If you cannot come upon a wise, mature companion whose ways are virtuous, you must go about life all alone, like a king who, abandoning his conquered kingdom, lives in exile, or like the elephant Mātanga who roams about the forest living in solitude.

VERSE 330

Better it is to live alone, for with a fool there is no fellowship. No evils do, be free of care, fare as a lone elephant in the wilds.

Q.4 Who is an Awake Person?

Dhammapada Verse 387: The sun is bright by day, the moon shines by night, the warrior is bright in his armor, the Brahmana is bright in his meditation; but the Buddha, the awakened, in his glory shines at all times, by day and by night.

The seeker who starts the search of Self by turning the extroverted senses in an inward direction becomes an awake person. **An awake person looks at the world with the eyes of the Soul, not with the eyes of the Ego.** Such a person can reach the inner self, and inner knowledge will manifest that the inner self and the entire Universe are connected. With awakening, your consciousness will expand, bringing along with it a sense of observation; you become a witness of how things are manifesting around you and what connection they have. **An awake person is more at peace with himself since he becomes the witness with no ego and fewer expectations attached.** He will master the art of Surrendering to The Universe's will. An awake person shines from afar, like the snowy mountains.

<u>Persian Proverb</u>

"**He who knows not,** and **knows not** that **he knows not,** is a fool, shun him; **He who knows not,** and **knows** that **he knows not,** is a child, teach **him. He who knows,** and **knows not** that **he knows,** is asleep, wake **him. He who knows,** and **knows** that **he knows,** is wise, follow **him.**"

Q.5 Who is a prudent person?

A prudent person takes no shame in asking about what he doesn't know.

A prudent person follows the path of truth and follows his heart, for he knows his soul is eternal and only goodness will fetch him eternal peace and bliss. A prudent person is thus guided to do whatever best he can in any circumstance of life. A prudent person will know the importance of a calm mind and discretion. He learns to look beyond the veil of illusion and see through intentions. His actions shall not be driven by hastiness or impulsiveness, rather by restraint and logic. He will be able to draw himself out of any difficult situation or dangers like an elephant sunk in mud using forbearance and wisdom.

We can heed the words of the wisest man who ever lived, King Solomon. "The prudent see danger and take refuge, but the simple keep going and pay the penalty" (Proverbs 27:12).

The simple person can also see the danger but doesn't take steps to combat those changes in time. He lacks the foresightedness to fathom the long-term implications of the consequences. Just recognizing the change and danger is not enough. To be successful in life, one must not only recognize the change but also change their strategy to deal with it so as to safeguard oneself and avoid danger. One needs prudence in life to deal with the ever-changing nature of life. *If one is sharp but has a complacent approach, it won't help them in any way. If one is not prudent, then he will have no choice but to repent later for not taking the right step on time.* You must do something about it. A prudent person discerns what is a right act and acts upon it. You need to take steps to deal with it lest you only live with regrets. It can be a relationship decision, a career choice, or any financial decision. The Universe can only give you a keen eye to see the far-reaching consequences but only your prudence can help you to reach your desired outcome by using your wisdom and experience. Life is too short to keep on repeating the same mistakes and not learn from past experiences. Thus, a prudent person uses the power of discernment on time and acts upon it.

Proverbs 27:12

A prudent *man* foresees the evil, *and* hides himself; *but* the simple pass on, *and* are punished.

Q.6 Who is a strong-minded person?

"The strong-minded will not faint, even when all is lost; the elephant stands firm, even when wounded by a shower of arrows."

- Thirukkural

A mentally strong person grows out of tough or stressful experiences rather than being bogged down by them. They have complete confidence in their capabilities and values. They know the power of their spirit and the power of the Universe, for they know situations will arise in life that will cause difficulties but that won't dampen their spirit as they live by the word of the Almighty. They will not seek validation from outside. Strong people don't need other people's approval, and they go forward in life and don't get discouraged. They don't let the naysayers hinder their progress. If you have a strong mind, you will focus only on reaching the goals of continuous growth, learning, and achievement.

A strong-minded person has a clear purpose in head which is completely aligned with their set of values. He is highly introspective and listens to their emotions and soul calling. They wear honesty and vulnerability as their armor - meaning that they have the mental buffer to not lie to people, to be authentic, and to disclose their feelings to the people around them without fearing rejection. They have learned to nourish their spirit over time and value their own freedom of emotional expression over people-pleasing and emotional suppression.

Mentally strong without being emotionally strong is like rich soil without flowers. Mentally and spiritually strong people don't take life or even small steps of progress for granted. They appreciate life and don't waste their lives in bickering, criticizing, or blaming. They know that only grace and gratitude can open the doors to new breakthroughs, possibilities, power, wisdom, and creativity within the Universe.

To be a strong-minded person, push forward against all the odds. Don't give in to fear or doubt and have firm faith that everything will work its way out sooner or later. A strong person surrounds themselves with nothing but positivity and love and reflects love and compassion back into the world - for they know that this holds the key to an abundant and loving life. Learn from an elephant. An elephant is large enough to do a great deal of damage; they aren't overtly destructive. They are not violent toward other creatures and, in spite of their size and strength, they have the power to be helpful and compassionate. By having open hearts and minds, we can create strong relationships within the community, therefore building a strong community.

Q.7. Who is Free from Pain?

Verse 361: Restraint in the body is good, good is restraint in speech; restraint in the mind is good, good is restraint in all the senses. A bhikkhu restrained in all the senses is freed from all ills (Samsara dukkh) – Dhammapada

Watchfulness over the senses along with the ability to enjoy one's own company will be free from pain. **Pain is never external; it is always internal**. No person or situation can inflict pain upon you unless you allow them to. If you can delight in your own company, if you can be your guide then no pain can sustain. It will pass away like a storm, and you will stand firm if your roots are deep. Even the greatest of windstorms cannot make them unstable. This depth comes from inner work – *when you dive deep within to introspect and realize your true power. Water your spirit from time to time to make your roots strong.* When your soul is parched and spirit is dry, devoid of love and compassion, nothing—absolutely nothing—can relieve the dry brittleness within you except the divine grace of God and guidance of the Universe. Ask the Universe or God to quench your spiritual thirst and irrigate the dry ground of your spirit. Only the nectar of love can free you from pain. A love that is so deep that nothing can mar the spirit of life within you. The deeper the love for the Divine, the more the gratefulness toward that Supreme power for creating a person like you, gifting a life so precious, endowing you with so many gifts…more you will fall in love with yourself and life. You will start seeing every pain as a test of that Supreme Power to help you become a finer person and aid you in understanding the true meaning of life. **A stronger person comes out beautifully out of every pain as a much more refined and better version of himself.**

People around you should wonder how a storm or pain that was meant to break you, shake you and uproot you could actually turn advantageous to you and you came out as a victorious warrior, a much brighter and cheerful person. Isn't that thought beautiful? Pain in life is inevitable but a person always has the choice to break the shackles of pain and free himself from suffering. Let the suffering slide by. **Do not be a victim of your mind or a slave of your mind. Conquer it with awareness: awareness of the ephemeral nature of difficult circumstances in one's life.** People leave. People change. You lose loved ones, jobs, or a home. You can get ill. You suffer losses. You may feel alone. This is life. This hurts.

But this is all ephemeral. Do not surrender under a sea of pressure and chaos. You can free yourself from pain, put yourself back together and turn over a new leaf with awareness of your emotions and challenging yourself that the only way after rock bottom is up, up and up. The key to a new happier life free from suffering lies with you. Trust the calling of your heart, let your soul illuminate the new way to approach life wherein you have a firm faith in the Divine that when pain hits, He will carry you and comfort you to help you restart the right way.

HOW

QUESTIONS TO HELP YOU ON YOUR PATH TO

AWARENESS AND ENLIGHTENMENT

HOW

Q.1 How to judge the character of a person?

"Consider a man's good qualities, and consider his faults; and judge his character by that which is more."
– Thiruvalluvar, Thirukkural

In life, the most important choices you make are related to people. You can make better decisions when you have the power or a keen eye to accurately judge the personality of others. *If you can make an accurate judgment about the integrity and character of a person, it may help you make more accurate judgments in life.* Character is the reflection of one's mind and soul. Intentions of a person define him. Words are very expressive of intents, including hidden and ulterior motives. Unlike words or stated intentions, actions reveal how a person consistently responds to different situations. **There's a saying in Taoism that no one can lie because the truth can be read in their intention for speaking.** Listen to what they have to say and look carefully at what they do. So, always judge a person by their words and actions. Is there congruence or consistency between their words and actions? The actions of a person must match their words if their character is strong. According to Immanuel Kant, a good action is motivated by duty and respect for moral law, rather than personal gain or emotions. To evaluate someone's character from a Kantian perspective, you might consider their motives — are they helping someone because it's genuinely the right thing to do, or for approval or advantage? Look for the good qualities they possess and the intentions.

A part of their character is revealed not only by their intentions but by the quality of their heart. Before you judge the character, observe the behavior of the person, get to know them, try to look beyond what is obvious, and ask these questions regarding that person -

- Do they have a clean heart?
- Do they feel a sense of embarrassment in doing wrong or after doing wrong unintentionally?
- Do they repent for their mistakes made when they were unaware?
- Do they believe in being truthful?
- Do they aim to help people when needed and asked?
- Do they show empathy to people when they suffer?
- Is there a heart full of love and compassion?
- Are they devoid of false pride?
- Are they respectful toward their inferiors?
- Are they honest?
- Are they kind to people in general?
- Do they have the virtues of patience, resilience, and forgiveness?
- Are they careful, efficient, organized, and vigilant in your efforts, based on your own principles or sense of what is right?
- Do they show respect toward the relationships they form and value them?
- Do they have good habits in life?
- Do they have goodwill in society?
- Do good people want to associate with them?
- Do they make good use of power, or abuse power?

However, it is a little difficult for an individual to possess all these qualities at any one point in time since character building is a lifelong process. But the core of a person should be fair and clean. If a person has even some of these qualities at a given time, then the person has a fairly good character. Observing someone's actions, understanding their motives, looking for empathy, and seeing consistency in their values can help us appreciate their character beyond surface impressions. However, it's also wise to remember that character is shaped by context, growth, and change, and may not always be fully visible to others. You can make better choices in life and avoid a lot of mishaps if you connect with the right people with strong character.

Q.2 How to discover your true self?

If you want to live a fulfilling life, you must first know who you truly are; this is something that takes searching to discover. It never happens when you're stuck in *fear* or doubt, and it certainly doesn't happen when you're numb and disconnected from yourself.

> "At the center of your being,
> You have the answer;
> You know who you are.
> and you know what you want."
>
> — Lao Tzu

You have to connect inwards to know your true self. There is a world inside you waiting to be explored. But you are always busy with the noise of the outside world. Until and unless you pay attention to your core or inner self, you cannot decipher the messages of your soul. Your soul wants to whisper to you, but are you ready to listen?

Do you pay attention to the messages it is trying to send you?

Do you listen carefully to that inner voice?

If you want to make good choices in life, you have to discover your true self. You need to be in a loving relationship with yourself first. What happens when we love someone is that we try to get to know that person better. We try to know their likes, dislikes, tastes, and preferences. We try to understand their beliefs and value system to connect with them. Then why do we not try to understand ourselves? If you want to connect with your true self, the answer is simple: start loving yourself. You need to start establishing a connection with yourself. Love yourself so much that you know everything about you.

- What drives you?
- What are your ideals and values?
- What makes you happy?
- What calms you down?
- What bothers you?
- What factors motivate you?
- What is your passion?
- What are your thought patterns, emotions, and sensations as they arise, and becoming aware of what you are bringing into each situation?

In order to find yourself, you have to be so in love with yourself and the process of finding your true self that you are ready to dig deep or mine to find the diamond – your soul or atman. It requires persistence and a lot of self-awareness. You have to be fully aware of what fabric your soul is made of. Each individual is different. To find a connection with your soul, you must be persistent in self-awareness, accountability, and take time to listen to the soul's desires. Dig through the rubble to find the treasure hidden within you. The rubble is of ego. As ego thins out, you get closer to the soul. The ego can make you disillusioned and play tricks, but your soul has all the answers. Just like an onion has layers, humans have layers too. You have to peel step by step with complete awareness to uncover your true self.

Meditation is a great way to connect with your inner self. It will awaken you when you embrace silence. We definitely live in a chaotic world, but not necessarily do we need to adapt to this chaotic energy. Silence can give you answers which you can find nowhere. Sometimes solitude is good. A lot of people fear solitude…those who fear solitude are restless souls. If you ask me, solitude is bliss. When you are silent, you observe more and judge less. It opens your mind with an intellectual curiosity, and your inner voice starts speaking to you. It will guide you in the right direction to help you make better decisions which are in alignment with your higher self.

"Through the portals of silence, the healing sun of wisdom and peace will shine upon you." - Paramahansa Yogananda.

In other words, less confusion, less self-doubt, less frustrated snapping at others from bottling things up, and much clearer personal boundaries, and more honest communication.

Your heart is the size of the ocean. Go find yourself in its hidden depths. - Rumi

Q.3 How to Be Hopeful in Stressful Times?

Hope is a beautiful thing to hold onto in life. The secret of living life beautifully is that you never take setbacks to heart and keep the flame of hope alive in your heart. Trust that there is a higher power which can help you, guide you, and ferry you through difficult times. Setbacks are a natural part of life, but they don't define us. Instead of allowing them to weigh heavily on our hearts, we can view them as learning opportunities. Each challenge we face can teach us valuable lessons, foster growth, and strengthen our resolve.

Trusting in a Higher Power

Believing in a higher power, whether that's a spiritual belief, the Universe, or a sense of purpose, can provide immense comfort to you. This trust will instill a sense of security, reminding us that you are not alone in your struggles. **It encourages you to surrender control over what you cannot change and to find peace in the journey, knowing that support is available.**

Trust in the Lord with all your heart.

and lean not on your own understanding;

In all your ways, submit to him,

and he will make your paths straight.

As you grow in the qualities of endurance and character, you build a foundation of genuine hope—an unshakable confidence in God's love and the anticipation of His promises. Hope is a powerful resource that is the result of tested and proven endurance and character. Hope is and can be your sure footing when life seems slippery, based on the certainty that even in the hardest of times, God has not forsaken us (Hebrews 13:5).

Place your trust and hope in God not on people. Trust and hope are deeply intertwined. When you trust someone, you're essentially placing your faith in their reliability and intentions, which naturally fosters hope for a positive outcome. This hope can provide comfort, especially in challenging situations, as it reinforces the belief that the person will come through for you. So, you put that faith and trust in a higher power.

"When you come to the edge of all that you know, you must believe in one of two things: either there will be land to stand on, or you will be given wings to fly." - Unknown

Keeping the Flame Alive

Keeping hope alive requires intentionality. Here are a few ways to nurture that flame:

1. **Practice Gratitude**: Regularly acknowledging what you're thankful for helps shift focus from what's lacking to what's abundant in your life.

2. **Surround Yourself with Positivity**: Engage with uplifting people, inspiring stories, and environments that nurture hope.

3. **Visualize Your Goals**: Create a vision board or write down your aspirations. Visualizing your goals reinforces your belief in a brighter future.

4. **Embrace Mindfulness**: Stay present and appreciate the small joys in life. Mindfulness helps maintain a hopeful outlook by anchoring us in the moment.

5. **Reflect on Past Resilience**: Remind yourself of previous challenges you've overcome. This reflection can bolster your confidence in facing current obstacles.

Story

In a quaint village, a revered sage named Ani often shared teachings from Hindu mythology. One evening, he spoke of **Arjuna,** the great warrior from the *Mahabharata,* who faced despair on the battlefield. Overwhelmed by doubt and fear, he hesitated to fight against his own kin. In that moment of crisis, Lord Krishna reminded him of his duty and purpose, urging him to embrace his strength. "Just as Arjuna learned," Ani said, "**We too must confront our fears and embrace our responsibilities. Hope is not just waiting for things to get better; it's about taking action, guided by our values and beliefs. In every challenge, remember that divine support and inner strength are always within reach.**" The villagers left with a renewed sense of purpose, ready to face their struggles with courage and hope.

Q.4 How to keep moving and growing?

Everything happens by God's will Nothing is beyond His reach or knowledge, making every event part of His divine plan. Every event is interconnected and plays a role in the broader cosmic design. Even the actions of individuals are seen as part of this tapestry, meaning that every decision and occurrence has a ripple effect that aligns with divine will.

Krishna says, "The whole cosmic order is under Me. Under My will, it is automatically manifested again and again, and under My will, it is annihilated at the end." - Bg 9.8

God is all-powerful and causes everything that happens in the world. Nothing happens without His willing it. But does that mean you leave everything to Him and become complacent? To be ready for what He wills, you need to prepare, you need to be inspired to work with devotion. You need to be ready to receive all that is ordained by Him. In Jewish thought, the concept of *Hashgacha Pratit* refers to God's personal involvement in the world. This belief asserts that God is aware of and oversees every detail of creation, ensuring that nothing happens without His consent. This perspective encourages believers to recognize the divine hand in all aspects of life, from the smallest events to significant occurrences.

You need to keep moving, transform yourself in order to evolve. It is called **The law of evolution** which will help you to move to a higher level of satisfaction by developing consciousness. The concept of the law of evolution suggests that personal growth is a natural and essential part of life, guiding us toward higher levels of satisfaction through the development of consciousness. *Embracing this journey means continuing to move forward, even in the face of difficulties. Challenges serve as catalysts for growth, offering valuable lessons that foster resilience and deeper insight.* As we navigate through life, we progress from innocence to ignorance and ultimately to wisdom. This evolution emphasizes the importance of reflection and learning from our experiences, transforming struggles into stepping stones for greater understanding. Ultimately, the idea of continuous movement encourages us to view change not as a setback but as an opportunity for ongoing personal and spiritual development.

Imagine you're going through a challenging time, whether it's a personal setback or a goal you haven't reached yet:

- **Trust** yourself to handle the situation and make the best decisions you can with what you know.

- **Faith** that this difficulty is part of your greater journey, and it's leading you toward growth or a deeper understanding.

- **Surrender** the need to control every detail, trusting that life will unfold in its own way and that things will get better when the time is right.

- **Patience** in the process, knowing that growth and success often take time and that rushing or forcing things may cause more harm than good.

Q.5 How to Deal with Disappointment or Hopelessness?

Key: Bhagavad Gita teaches us the importance of remaining steady and focused amidst the ups and downs of life. Lord Krishna implores that by adopting an attitude of detachment toward success and failure, we can maintain our peace of mind and navigate life's challenges with grace and resilience. **Grace** and **Resilience** become the key words here.

Your failure or disappointments are a way for the Universe to show you a different path to success. In times of hopelessness, be graceful and accept the situation for what it is.

Chapter 2, Verse 38, Gita

सुखदुःखे समे कृत्वा लाभालाभौ जयाजयौ।

ततो, युद्धाय, युज्यस्व, नैवं, पापमवाप्स्यसि ॥ 38॥

Sukha-duḥkhe same kṛitvā, lābhālābhau jayājayau.

Tato yuddhāya yujyasva, naivaṁ pāpam avāpsyasi.

Success unbalances the mind by a wave of over-excitement, and defeat by a wave of depression or hopelessness. But Lord Krishna tells us to remain equanimous by having an equal mind in pain and pleasure, gain and loss, victory and defeat, engaging in battle, and thereby you will not incur sin.

When you adopt the principle of equanimity or samatvam, a grace enters your intellect. You do not become disheartened so easily. It is a life-changing skill. You accept everything, be it success or failure, gracefully. You do not get swayed by good experiences; you are not attached to them so that when you face bad times, you are not in deep despair, you remain grounded. You do not linger after the good times' experiences only; rather, you remain calm. You will not react instantly. This will help you in seeing the complete picture and help you in adopting a far-sighted approach. You are steady in your approach in life, and nothing can dampen your spirit. You become a developed soul who has a fair understanding of inner peace, resilience, grace, and divine will be with him, being a 'Nimitta' or an instrument of work. Life is a play, and we all are characters doing our role.

So, rise above the never-ending desires by fixing your consciousness on the Lord. Become your own master by controlling your senses.

"Rely on God, and you will find strength not only to endure the storms of life but also to grow in the beauty of His grace."

Spiritual Guidance

- If friends and relatives become enemies and leave one to suffer alone?

- If you are facing financial problems or health problems?

If all other means and support vanish and one has no one to look at. If in such a distressful condition one remembers the merciful Waheguru (through the true Naam of course), then even hot air cannot touch one. **So powerful is Naam.**

- **Asa Di Var**: In this hymn, Guru Nanak speaks about the ups and downs of life, encouraging listeners to remain steadfast in faith and to recognise that God is always with us. Read the words from it.

  o **Line**: "Sabh Bhao Kaun Hoi, Jit Deen Dukh Daai."

  o **Meaning**: All fear is dispelled when one seeks refuge in God. It reminds us that God is the ultimate support during hardships.

- **Raag Malaar** (Ang 1282):

  o **Line**: "Dukh Laghai Ta Dukh Mitaai."

  o **Meaning**: When suffering arises, remember the Divine to alleviate pain. This underscores the role of remembrance in healing.

- **Raag Tukhari** (Ang 1008):

  o **Line**: "Man tu Karta, Tera Nao."

  o **Meaning**: O mind, remember your Creator. This encourages a focus on the Divine to overcome feelings of despair.

Japji Sahib (First Pauri):

This Shabad emphasizes the importance of remembering the Divine and the power of Naam. It highlights that true peace comes from connecting with Waheguru. Feel the essence of these beautiful lines.

Sochai soch na hova-ee jay sochee lakh vaar.

Chupai chup na hova-ee jay laaye rahaa liv taar.

Bhukhiaa bhukh na utree jay banna pureeaa bhaar.

Sahas siaannpaa lakh hoeh ta ik na chalai naal.

Kiv sachiaaraa hoeeai kiv koorrai tuttai paal.

Hukam rajaa-ee chalnnaa Naanak likhiaa naal. ||1||

By thinking, the True One cannot be reduced to thought,

even by thinking hundreds of thousands of times.

By remaining silent, inner silence is not obtained,

even by remaining lovingly absorbed deep within.

The hunger of the hungry is not appeased,

even by piling up loads of worldly goods.

There are hundreds of thousands of clever tricks,

But not even one of them will go along with you in the end.

So, how can you become truthful?

And how can the veil of illusion be torn away?

O Nanak, it is written that you shall obey the Command of the True One,

and walk in the way of the Divine Will.

Q.7 How to deal with people who don't value you?

There are people who don't value you, ridicule you, manipulate you to fit into their ideal image. No matter what you do, they will end up emptying your emotional reserves too. **Sometimes, even if you are a sensible person, you seem to lose it**. It starts affecting you. Somewhere or the other, you start becoming like them. If someone constantly ridicules you, you will end up defending yourself more by being harsh or answering them in their language. In the whole process, what you lose is your integrity, and you sway from your dharma.

"The Best Revenge Is Not to Be Like Your Enemy" (Marcus Aurelius). You should not enter the mud to fight. Stay away from negative people. By all means, they can try to portray you as the worst person or the one who is wrong. But you should not lose your track and become one of them.

If someone doesn't value you, that shows their sense of low self-worth. Have you heard of the term candle blower? They are the people who don't want to see you thrive. They will deliberately demean you, gossip about you, and try to bring you down. So, your value depends on you and only you. Let your light shine, be exuberant, be vivacious. Be yourself.

Your inner light will shine when you are at peace with yourself. *'Never lose your inner light, the light of goodness, of love; the light of an open warm heart.'* - *Dalai Lama*

Remember

When the door to a toxic relationship closes, the Universe opens a window or another door to a more life-giving connection. The opening can be immediate; at other times, there can be a waiting period.

Q.8 How Can I Align My Actions with My Spiritual Values?

Aligning Actions with Spiritual Values: A Journey Toward Fulfillment

Finding meaning in life often leads us to seek a deeper alignment between our actions and our spiritual values. This journey goes beyond following rules; it's about discovering what truly fulfills us. Aristotle wisely said, "Knowing yourself is the beginning of all wisdom." By understanding our core values— like compassion, integrity, humility, and service—we can navigate life's complexities with greater purpose.

The *Tao Te Ching* reminds us, "When you realize nothing is lacking, the whole world belongs to you." This idea suggests that when our actions resonate with our spiritual values, we experience a profound sense of fulfillment. Aligning our actions with our values becomes a personal journey that also positively impacts the world around us.

The Power of Intention

To achieve this alignment, being intentional about our choices is essential. In the *Bhagavad Gita*, we learn that "Whatever action a man performs, he should be unselfish and devoted to the Supreme." This means that acting with a clear purpose can guide us toward making choices that benefit not just ourselves but others as well. There was a young man named Arin who, after much internal conflict, chose to dedicate his life to helping the poor in his community. His unwavering intention to serve transformed not only his life but also the lives of many he encountered. This is the power of intention.

The Role of Mindfulness

Mindfulness is another key element in this process. In the practice of mindfulness, we realize that every moment holds the potential for joy if we take the time to notice. Practicing mindfulness allows us to be aware of our thoughts and actions, enabling us to respond to situations with clarity.

A powerful story illustrates this: a monk was walking through the forest when he encountered a struggling traveler. Instead of rushing past, he paused to help the traveler carry his heavy load. By being present and mindful, the monk not only alleviated the traveler's burden but also experienced joy in the act of service. This awareness helps ensure that we act in ways aligned with our spiritual beliefs, fostering deeper integrity.

Embracing Challenges

However, the journey toward alignment isn't always easy. The old Chinese proverb, "The journey of a thousand miles begins with a single step," reminds us that growth takes time. We will face moments when our actions don't match our values. Instead of viewing these moments as failures, we can see them as valuable opportunities for reflection and growth.

The Importance of Community

Creating a supportive community is also vital. The saying "It takes a village to raise a child" applies to spiritual growth as well. Surrounding ourselves with people who share our values creates an encouraging environment where we can hold each other accountable.

The teachings of the Buddha emphasize the importance of *sangha*, or community. A story from his life tells of how he built a community of monks and laypeople who supported each other in their spiritual journeys. This collective effort not only strengthened individual resolve but also fostered a sense of belonging and shared purpose.

Finding Meaning in Everyday Actions

"He who has a why to live can bear almost any how." This highlights the importance of connecting our everyday actions to our deeper spiritual values. When we anchor our decisions in this broader purpose, we build resilience and meaning.

Take the story of Mother Teresa, who dedicated her life to serving the poorest of the poor in India. Despite facing immense challenges and hardships, her unwavering commitment to her mission brought comfort and hope to countless individuals. Her life exemplifies how aligning actions with spiritual values can create a ripple effect of positive change.

Celebrating Small Wins

Celebrating small wins is crucial, too. The saying "Little by little, one travels far" reminds us to recognize our progress, no matter how small. Each step taken in line with our spiritual values strengthens our foundation and inspires those around us.

Consider the story of a young girl who, each day, made it a point to help someone in her neighborhood—whether it was sharing her lunch with a friend or assisting an elderly neighbor with groceries. Over time, her small acts of kindness created a wave of goodwill that transformed her community.

Conclusion

In conclusion, aligning our actions with our spiritual values is an ongoing journey that requires intention, mindfulness, and community. By reflecting on ourselves, taking purposeful actions, and embracing the challenges we face, we can live with integrity and authenticity. As we embark on this journey, let's remember the age-old wisdom: "What we think, we become." By consciously choosing to embody our values, we create lives that resonate with our spiritual essence, leading to true fulfillment and harmony. This journey encourages us not just to exist but to live fully and meaningfully, contributing to the collective tapestry of humanity. Every small, conscious step taken with intention and authenticity ripples outward, creating a positive impact. Let us commit to living with purpose, knowing that the way we align our actions with our spiritual values shapes not only our own journey, but also the collective evolution of humanity.

Shine your light, not for the world to see, but for the world to feel.

Final Words

Dearest Reader

As we come to the close of this journey, remember that life's greatest traps are often those we create within ourselves. We become ensnared in fears of the future, regrets of the past, judgments of others, and self-doubt. But true freedom, the freedom we have been seeking, lies in choosing to live beyond these traps. It lies in embracing the present with acceptance, in facing each day with courage, and in seeking truth within our own hearts.

Enlightened living is not a destination but a way of being, a continuous unfolding, where peace is found not in perfect circumstances but in a deep acceptance of what is. Release the need for answers, let go of striving for constant improvement, and instead, awaken to the fullness of each moment. This is where life truly lives.

May this book serve as a reminder to honor each step of your journey, to live with an open heart and an open mind, and to see yourself and others with compassion and understanding. Beyond all traps, beyond all illusions, there is only this: the eternal presence of your own awareness. Return to it whenever you stray, for it is your truest home.

Above all, may you come to see that life itself is a profound gift. Every moment holds the potential for love. Every breath is a chance to start anew. Enlightened living is not reserved for a chosen few; it is the birthright of every human being who is willing to open their heart to life. Your destiny is not to become something other than what you are but to peel away all that is false so that your truest essence can shine forth.

As you close this book, let it be the beginning of your own journey to freedom. You are the creator of your path, the architect of your destiny, and the keeper of a light that can illuminate not only your life but the lives of others. Live in such a way that your very presence becomes a source of peace, joy, and inspiration to those around you. This is the gift of enlightened living.

So walk forward, boldly yet gently. Carry these words with you, but more importantly, carry the quiet wisdom of your own heart. Let each day bring you closer to the realization that your truest destiny is not to seek perfection but to live fully and freely, in harmony with all that is. May you find peace within, may you live with courage, and may you reach your truest destiny, not somewhere out there, but here, in each sacred moment of your life.

Walk forward in peace, in clarity, and in love. May you live each day enlightened and free.

Love and Light

Mandakini Tomar

Bibliography

Does Guru Granth Sahib describe depression? - PMC (nih.gov)

Indian J Psychiatry. 2013 Jan; 55 (Suppl 2): S195–S200.

doi: *10.4103/0019-5545.105531*

PMCID: PMC3705682

PMID: *23858254*

Does *Guru Granth Sahib* describe depression?

Gurvinder Kalra, Kamaldeep Bhui,[1] and *Dinesh Bhugra*[2]